THE RETIREMENT CHALLENGE: WILL YOU SINK OR SWIM?

THE RETIREMENT CHALLENGE: WILL YOU SINK OR SWIM?

A Complete, Do-It-Yourself
Toolkit to Navigate Your
Financial Future

Frank Armstrong, III
with Jason R. Doss

Vice President, Publisher: Tim Moore
Associate Publisher and Director of Marketing: Amy Neidlinger
Executive Editor: Jim Boyd
Editorial Assistant: Myesha Graham
Development Editor: Russ Hall
Operations Manager: Gina Kanouse
Digital Marketing Manager: Julie Phifer
Publicity Manager: Laura Czaja
Assistant Marketing Manager: Megan Colvin
Cover Designer: Alan Clements
Managing Editor: Kristy Hart
Project Editor: Anne Goebel
Copy Editor: Water Crest Publishing
Proofreader: Kathy Ruiz
Indexer: Erika Millen
Compositor: TnT Design, Inc.
Manufacturing Buyer: Dan Uhrig
© 2009 by Pearson Education, Inc.
Publishing as FT Press
Upper Saddle River, New Jersey 07458

FT Press offers excellent discounts on this book when ordered in quantity for bulk purchases
or special sales. For more information, please contact U.S. Corporate and Government Sales,
1-800-382-3419, corpsales@pearsontechgroup.com. For sales outside the U.S., please contact
International Sales at international@pearson.com.

Printed in the United States of America
Second Printing April 2009
ISBN-10: 0-13-236132-9
ISBN-13: 978-0-13-236132-3
Pearson Education LTD.
Pearson Education Australia PTY, Limited.
Pearson Education Singapore, Pte. Ltd.
Pearson Education North Asia, Ltd.
Pearson Education Canada, Ltd.
Pearson Educatión de Mexico, S.A. de C.V.
Pearson Education—Japan
Pearson Education Malaysia, Pte. Ltd.
Library of Congress Cataloging-in-Publication Data
Armstrong, Frank, III.
   The retirement challenge: will you sink or swim? : a complete, do-it-yourself toolkit to
navigate your financial future / Frank Armstrong with Jason R. Doss.
     p. cm.
   ISBN-10: 0-13-236132-9 (pbk. : alk. paper)
   ISBN-13: 978-0-13-236132-3
   1. Retirement--United States. 2. Older people--United States--Finance, Personal. I. Doss,
Jason R. II. Title.
   HQ1064.U5A755 2009
   332.024'014--dc22
                              2008029134

For
Absent Comrades
and
All the Sailors Still at Sea

Contents

Contributed by Jason Doss

Acknowledgments

No one writes a book like this alone. This work has been one giant collective effort by many talented people, whose patience I probably have severely strained on occasion.

Barbara Hendra, my agent and public relations consultant, reversed the natural order of things by selling the book before I ever thought about writing it. Then, when your author faltered, she provided encouragement, invaluable organizational guidance, and editorial support to whip the manuscript into shape.

Jason Doss took time from his day job as one of America's leading investor advocates to provide real life vignettes where things went horribly wrong with the advice Wall Street provided, and to point out that investors have recourse when their advisors betray their trust.

My professional associates at Investor Solutions, Inc. run our day to day operations flawlessly, freeing up my time to think, speak, and write on subjects dear to my heart. Perhaps they just enjoy having me out of their hair so they can take proper care of our clients. If so, they are kind enough not to say so.

The experience working with the FT Press team couldn't have been more pleasant. Jim Boyd encouraged me and provided guidance at critical stages in the development of the manuscript. If ever a man deserved the description "unflappable," it is him.

My wife, Gabriele, put up with me when I was cranky, distracted, or frustrated during the laborious process of writing, rewriting, and editing the project. How she stays so cheerful is a source of constant amazement.

When mistakes happen, it's always comforting to find someone else to blame. But, unfortunately, I alone am responsible for any errors that survived the team's diligent scrutiny.

Thank you all for your support, encouragement, guidance, and good humor.

About the Authors

Frank Armstrong, III, CLU, CFP™, AIF, is the founder and principal of Investor Solutions, Inc., a fee-only registered investment advisor. He has more than 30 years' experience in the securities and financial services industry. His bestselling book *The Informed Investor* was cited by *BusinessWeek* as one of the best investment books of the year. Frank was named by *Barron's* as one of the top 100 independent financial advisors in 2007 and again in 2008. He was a featured columnist on Morningstar.com for a number of years and is a frequent contributor to AccountsWorld.com and FundsInteractive.com. He has appeared on "CNN Headline News," "Your Money with Stewart Varney," "PBS Morning Business Report," CNBC, "Money Life with Chuck Jaffee," and public radio stations around the country. Frank is widely quoted in the media, his articles appear in major financial magazines and Web sites, and he lectures nationwide on principles of investment management.

Jason R. Doss is an attorney and a partner with the Atlanta-based law firm, Page Perry, LLC. He represents consumers against the financial services industry in securities arbitrations and consumer class action litigation. Jason has a proven track record of fighting for consumers' rights and for taking major corporations to task. Over the last few years, he has initiated some of the largest consumer class action cases in the country. Since 2001, Jason has been an active member of the Public Investors Arbitration Bar Association (PIABA), a national organization devoted to representing investors in securities arbitration. He has held various positions, including Editor-In-Chief of the *PIABA Bar Journal*, a nationally recognized legal publication.

Introduction

Bill Gates and Warren Buffett are probably not stressing about their retirement income—but many Americans are. Study after study shows that they are not on track to support themselves in retirement and are behind their parents at the same age. Yet, most Americans spend more time researching which flat screen TV to buy than planning for retirement. Like Scarlett O'Hara in *Gone with the Wind*, they choose to "worry about that tomorrow."

I can guess some reasons why you might put off dealing with your retirement: it's not fun, it takes a long time, it's complicated, it's difficult, it's confusing—it's all the above! I sympathize. Really I do. But I don't believe it's any of those things. Well, OK, perhaps your version of fun is a little different from mine. But planning your retirement isn't an ordeal. It can be done quickly, elegantly, simply, and economically. Hang in there with me. I'm going to prove it to you.

My first book, *The Informed Investor*, delivered the Cliff Notes of an MBA investment class. I reviewed investment theory and practice as it developed over the last 50 years. I'm not going to do that again in this book, but if you feel the need for more background, I recommend *The Informed Investor*.

This time, I'm going to stick to practical, actionable information and strategies for retirement planning. If *The Informed Investor* was 90% theory and 10% action items, *The Retirement Challenge: Will You Sink or Swim?* is 90% specific information and action items. It gives you the tools to take control of your financial success without drowning in trivia or being overwhelmed by boring repetitive chores.

First, you meet your pension plan. You learn what it is, how to calculate benefits, how it works, what can go wrong, what to do if something goes wrong, and whether it's even attractive enough for you to participate. If it's not, you have viable alternatives and, under a 2008 U.S. Supreme Court Ruling, some recourse.

Next, wherever you are in your career, there are smart moves you want to pursue to maximize your retirement benefits. Whether you are right out of school, or already in retirement, you have lots of options to control your benefits.

How much will you need for retirement? Early in your career, it might be hard to estimate, but as you get closer, you can refine your guesstimate. You will learn how.

Finally, you learn how to invest your retirement assets economically and effectively while controlling risk to give yourself the highest probability of success in meeting your goals. Best of all, the system is easy to monitor and set up, and it works with all your investment accounts, whether inside a pension plan or your taxable accounts.

---

www.Sink-Swim.com

Do-It-Yourself

A companion Web site, www.Sink-Swim.com, provides you with a wealth of additional information and updates. Visit this Web site for the following:

- Hundreds of articles on investment theory, products, and best practices.
- Updates to pension law, regulation, and enforcement.
- Over 75 calculators that let you see how much you need to contribute for a prosperous retirement and whether you are on track to meet your goals.
- Sample asset allocation plans that can be adjusted for any stage of your career and portfolio size.
- Budget spreadsheets.
- Links to other useful sites.
- Discussion groups and a blog.
- A *Sink or Swim* newsletter.
- Exclusive Web bonus material: Estate planning issues with retirement accounts.

The Retirement Challenge: Will You Sink or Swim? is a reference work you can consult so when you have a retirement planning concern, you can identify it, understand it, take corrective action, and get back out on the golf course of life. For instance, if you are faced with a career change or forced early retirement, the sections in this book on changing jobs and IRA rollovers will be invaluable.

You might not need or even want to read every chapter word for word, or you might want to come back to some sections later. For instance, if you don't have a defined benefit pension plan, it won't wreck your life not to read that chapter. And if your primary concern is required minimum distributions for folks over 70½, reading the sections on early retirement tactics might not benefit you much. Feel free to pick and choose as your situation warrants.

Given the limited time most of us have and the various demands made upon our time, a system that requires minimum intervention and attention, yet still carry you to your goal, is the one that is most likely to be employed, and most likely to succeed. What's needed is an autopilot-type approach that is reasonably simple to set up and, once set up, will tend itself.

As a former airline pilot, I have a great appreciation for autopilots. By doing the grunt work of keeping the airplane in level flight headed in the right direction, autopilots free up the pilot for higher-level tasks, making aviation safer and more reliable. However, even the best autopilot needs to know where it's supposed to go and needs some degree of monitoring. Flight planning and situational awareness are still an important part of mission success. So, you can't bail out entirely, but you can limit your involvement to high-level planning and supervision.

Political correctness is not my strong suit. Everybody who knows me knows exactly how I feel about almost everything. You won't find me beating around many bushes. In particular, I believe that both the pension laws and the securities industry need major reform. They don't work as advertised to assist Americans to meet their legitimate financial goals. Advise your elected representatives that this is a critical issue that must be addressed. Let them know you are watching. In the meantime, you have to work with the current system and, if you understand it, you can pick and choose the parts that will work best for you—if you cherry-pick the system, you can make it work wonderfully.

In the spirit of full disclosure, my daytime job is providing investment advice. So, naturally I believe that competent, objective advisors add value. Not everyone shares that opinion, however. Some investors are determined to "go it alone." If you fit into this category, following the principles I present will improve your investment results. If you want to delegate to a professional, I'll lay out how to choose one that is both competent and objective.

During my occasional appearances as an expert witness in securities arbitration and litigation, and during Jason Doss's career as a plaintiff's attorney securities litigator, we get to see more than a few investment crashes. The vast majority should never have happened. Crashes happen when the investor or advisor violates important investment principles. By looking at how other people screwed up, you can reduce the chance of being the next victim. Jason Doss is one of America's brightest securities litigators. He provides a lot of our crash analysis in this book, so you can learn from other people's mistakes.

There really are sharks in the financial waters. And there are lifeguards. Unfortunately, sharks and lifeguards might look somewhat alike to the casual observer. One of the biggest mistakes investors make is trusting the wrong advisors. Jason has a lot of experience with the sharks. Although Jonah might have gotten off lucky with the whale, Jason is the first to admit it's hard to retrieve a swimmer once he's been eaten by a shark. Better to avoid them in the first place.

With millions of boomers approaching retirement, and trillions of dollars changing hands from pensions to the boomers, retirees are a

target-rich environment for the financial industry. Sharks circle endlessly, looking for that juicy, easily picked-off meal. Sharks don't have
morals; they just eat things that look tasty. Sharks have many distin-
guishing characteristics, however, and can rather easily be avoided if
you know how to spot them.

If you do get bitten by a shark, all might not be lost. Although
there are significant legal differences and performance expectations
between fiduciary advisors and salespeople, all financial advisors are
held to minimum standards of care and might be accountable for
losses that occurred as a result of their lapses. Recovering losses is an
uphill battle, however, so it's best to avoid the problem in the first
place. As Ben Franklin so aptly put it: "An ounce of prevention is better than a pound of cure."

As a lawyer who represents investors, I see firsthand what happens
when things go wrong. Even though the circumstances of each case
and client are different, they all have one thing in common: All of my
clients have lost money, trusting that their financial professional was
acting in their best interest. I am faced with the difficult task of trying
to get money back from brokerage firms, investment advisors, and
insurance companies. If Frank Armstrong is the swim instructor in
this analogy, then I am the paramedic. Most of the time, clients come
to my office because they have nowhere else to turn. Unfortunately,
though, most investors do not know that they can recover their losses
from financial advisors who give bad advice. Let me take this opportunity to correct a common misconception:

**Investing your money with a financial professional is not
gambling!**

If your trusted professional gives you bad advice, they (not you!) are
responsible for the losses, and the laws allow you to recover your damages from the financial advisors and their firms. However, you do not
want to rely on a paramedic to save your life. The best (and less
painful) approach is not to drown in the first place!

Frank Armstrong's vast knowledge and experience with financial issues and his no-nonsense style of writing is the best way to learn about these daunting issues. If you wait to hear the topics in this book for the first time from a broker (that is, a salesperson), you will undoubtedly turn into someone who doesn't ask questions and blindly follows the advice of a stranger with a likeable personality. That is the best way to drown and lose your hard-earned nest egg.

News flash: Sharks always smile before they bite! One of the biggest mistakes that I see investors make is that they do not do their homework before picking a financial professional or before agreeing to an investment strategy recommended by a trusted professional. The question of who is investing your money is just as important as how your money is invested. All too often, investors choose their advisor based solely on personality. This is a big mistake because con-artists or simply incompetent salespeople always have a likeable personality. Before picking an advisor, you must dig deeper into their background and be able to articulate your investment goals prior to your first meeting. This book helps you separate the experts from the idiots.

My goal for this book is to keep you from becoming a victim of a terrible financial experience, and to provide you with the practical tools that help you to sleep better at night, knowing that you are in control of your own financial future. At various places along the way, I provide real-life examples of what can happen if you are not prepared to tackle the financial issues that face millions of investors every day. These examples are meant to reinforce the lessons explained by Frank Armstrong.

—*Contributed by Jason Doss*

Part I

OVERVIEW OF THE RETIREMENT PROBLEM

Lesson 1————————————

You Are On Your Own

Americans traditionally expected defined benefit retirement plans, had networks of family support, looked forward to a rich Social Security benefit, and saved generously.

None of that is necessarily available to tomorrow's retirees. You must assume responsibility for your own retirement in the new era of cradle-to-grave insecurity. If you don't, nobody else is going to do it for you.

Surviving in an Era of Cradle-to-Grave Insecurity!

The days when all you needed to do was show up reasonably often and reasonably sober over the course of your career to earn a guaranteed income for life at retirement are over! In the good old days, the entire cost and responsibility for providing that retirement was assumed by the employer, as reflected in Table 1.1.

TABLE 1.1 Roles and Responsibilities: Defined Benefit Plans

Function	Employer	Employee
Determines benefit level	✔	
Calculates required contribution	✔	
Makes contributions	✔	
Makes investment decisions	✔	
Responsible for shortfall in capital	✔	
Pays plan administration cost	✔	
Converts account to lifetime income	✔	
Provides survivor benefit	✔	
Provides pre-retirement death benefit	✔	
Pays for investment advice	✔	
Provides education and advice	✔	

Under this type of plan, everything was done for you. You could be virtually brain dead and still expect a secure retirement.

Just 15 years ago, 70% of America's workers were covered by a defined benefit plan; all workers and their families were covered by a generous Social Security system. In our parents' time, the average employment was 25 years. Many employees had only one job their entire life; today, many people have a different job approximately every four years. Additionally, families were closer, and most expected to provide some intergenerational support. Even if this wasn't exactly cradle-to-grave security, it did take a lot of the uncertainty out of life.

That world doesn't exist anymore. Today, it's the Ownership Society—a euphemism for "sink or swim on your own resources." Depending on what type of organization you work for, the basic American retirement plan is now a 401(k), 403(b), or 457 plan. For-profit companies utilize 401(k) plans, whereas not-for-profit organizations have 401(k) or 403(b) plans, and state and municipal employees are covered by 457 plans or 401(k) plans. These plans are all very similar in that they require workers to decide on an adequate funding level, contribute all or most of that amount from their own pocket, develop a rational asset allocation plan, choose from a bewildering menu of substandard investment options, and, finally, determine how to convert their nest egg into a lifetime income. The employee-funded, employee-directed retirement is a new and disconcerting development.

Table 1.2 shows how the majority of responsibility shifts to the employee in the employee-funded plan (401[k], 403[b], and 457).

TABLE 1.2   Roles and Responsibilities: 401(k) and 403(b) Plans

Function	Employer	Employee
Determines benefit level		✔
Calculates required contribution		✔
Makes contribution	Matching contribution	✔
Makes investment decisions		✔
Responsible for shortfall in capital		✔
Pays plan administration cost	Rarely	✔
Converts account to lifetime income		✔
Provides survivor benefit	Account balance	✔
Provides pre-retirement death benefit		✔
Pays for investment advice		✔
Provides education and advice	Some	✔

No matter what happens to the current Social Security debate, benefits going forward (in real terms) will be a fraction of what our parents enjoyed. The national savings rate hovers near zero; during some months, it's negative. Average household savings for boomers is far too low to meet their retirement needs.

There's plenty of evidence that most Americans aren't up to the task of managing their retirement security. Workers are retiring earlier, often against their will. They are living longer and facing health costs that were unimaginable for their parents.

To put it kindly, the American pension system is one giant disaster area—a tsunami cresting over our heads. The time to take evasive action is now.

And help is not on the way! Investor literacy is almost nonexistent. You can graduate from high school without knowing how to balance your checkbook, graduate from college without ever taking an investment course, and get a PhD without ever hearing of asset allocation. Few accountants have ever studied portfolio construction, and most MBA programs and courses spend just one or two hours on the subject of portfolio construction.

The employee-funded retirement system—with some notable exceptions—is such a swamp that in many cases, the employee decides not to participate. Nationwide, it's an acknowledged failure. The system is plagued by high costs, poor investment choices, and insufficient education to enable employees to make informed decisions. As a result, it is little used. Many employees don't participate at all or fail to contribute enough to fund their retirement. Of those who do participate, many make consistently poor investment choices.

If the 401(k) system is a swamp, the 403(b) system is a sewer. Again, with some notable exceptions, it's a complete disaster for participants. However, it's a great way for unions and local governments to repay political favors and distant relatives. The kindest possible interpretation of the 403(b) system is that many of the people who administer it are hopelessly inept.

The great investment houses that might be expected to provide assistance are instead bent on the plunder and pillage of their clients' accounts. Wall Street's commission-based sales system is so corrupt, it can't be fixed. Not everybody at every brokerage is a crook, but the incentives are all wrong. The commission-crazed sales system taints the entire advice model. You can't rely on getting either competent or objective advice there.

The cops (both state and federal regulators) allow toxic products to foul the retirement system. Conflicts of interest and undisclosed costs are universally acknowledged and little punished.

So, there it is. You are entering an era of cradle-to-grave insecurity. You and only you are going to be responsible for securing your financial future. You are left to your own devices to figure out this system. That's what the Ownership Society is all about. You are not moving toward a kinder, gentler society. The safety net and lifeline are disappearing. You will either sink or swim depending on your own skill.

You are on your own. You must educate yourself, take responsibility for your financial future, and design and execute a viable investment plan for yourself. If you don't, it's highly doubtful that anybody else is going to do it for you.

Given all that, if you would like to survive in the new society, it's time for some swimming lessons—or maybe it's time for you to start building your very own life raft.

If you can't swim and suddenly find yourself alone in deep water, the last thing you want to hear is a detailed lecture on fluid mechanics or how to calculate buoyancy. Someday you might get interested in those subjects, but the immediate need is to keep your head above water and get yourself moving toward safety. Likewise, *The Retirement Challenge: Will You Sink or Swim?* is not going to turn you into a financial economist, accountant, or analyst. However, you will be able to invest your retirement accounts and personal savings simply, quickly, economically, and effectively to meet your long-term goals.

The Retirement Challenge: Will You Sink or Swim? will teach you those essential survival skills needed to navigate serenely to a safe harbor through the nastiest financial storms likely to be encountered on your journey.

Let me be completely clear. The author of this book is the swim coach. You are the swimmer. Reading this book will not make you financially secure. Learning everything about pensions will not lead to a prosperous retirement. Only saving and investing effectively will do it—and only you can make that happen.

Let's suspend disbelief for a second and pretend that you meet with the world's best investment advisor. If you don't have any capital, and you don't have the ability to save, the advisor can't do anything for

LESSON 1 • YOU ARE ON YOUR OWN

you. Without serious commitment on your part, you and the advisor have a pleasant conversation and you go on to be a financial failure.

It is ridiculously hard for anybody in reasonable health to drown in calm, warm water. It's a very benign environment. Almost everyone should be able to float for days and swim for many hours. You don't have to be strong, smart, or brave. Simply roll on your back, put your head down, relax, and breathe normally. You will float serenely. Then just kick a little and sweep your arms around to swim for miles. Arrive on that distant shore relaxed and refreshed.

And yet people do drown. Why? You would have to do just about everything wrong. Panic and lack of knowledge sink them. Drowning swimmers are often their own worst enemy. Instead of conserving energy and floating comfortably, the swimmers flail around in total panic, quickly exhausting themselves and insuring early demise. A tiny bit of knowledge and discipline would save them.

In the same manner, most investment tragedies are self-inflicted wounds—totally predictable, but completely avoidable. The world's stock and bond markets are remarkably benign. With just a little planning and minimal effort, you can confidently expect to have a comfortable and secure retirement.

Wall Street sharks are the most vicious kind, world famous for their remorseless search for unwitting prey. Fortunately, you don't have to be dinner for them. *The Retirement Challenge: Will You Sink or Swim?* provides you with tested repellent to fend off these dangerous critters.

The pace of modern life doesn't give you time to do all the things you "ought to" do. Unfortunately, most of us are swamped with competing obligations. The average American considers investment planning almost as much fun as doing taxes. But, taxes have an April 15th deadline and investment planning doesn't. So, it's far too easy to push the planning process to the back of the desk for another day. The danger is that it will linger there, gathering dust until you wake up one day to discover that time has passed you by, and you have neither a plan, nor any investments. So, the first goal of *The Retirement Challenge: Will You Sink or Swim?* is to make this process quick and easy so you can get on to the fun things in life, while knowing that you will probably be in the top quartile of investors over your career.

So, can retirement planning and investment be easy, simple to understand, painless and quick to execute, effective, and economical? The author guarantees it. Read on. *The Retirement Challenge: Will You Sink or Swim?* is your life vest in turbulent financial waters.

Lesson 2 ——————————————————

The Changing Face of Retirement

Retirement used to mean a short period between age 65 and death where the retiree sat on the front porch and vegetated.

Not anymore. Today, baby boomers are going in and out of the workforce, changing careers, going part-time, delaying retirement—many refuse to consider ever slowing down. Most of today's 60-year-olds are healthy, vigorous, and engaged. They have to plan for 40 years or more without a paycheck, while taking care of their parents, children, and grandchildren. Not all of them will make it that long, but they can't plan on anything less than age 95.

While walking down the docks in Bimini recently, the author of this book was hailed by a jolly young man of about 70, who was lounging comfortably on the back deck of his cruiser. Let's call him Walter. After the mandatory chit-chat that happens when boaters meet—consisting of complimenting each other on the boats, discussing the weather, fishing, maintenance, and how our trip was going—he volunteered that he was retired. So, of course, the author had to ask: "How's that working out for you?"

It turns out he loved it. He loved it so much, in fact, that this was the third time he had retired. His first retirement ended when he got bored. He fished so much, he became sick and tired of it. Even today, he won't throw a line in the water. His second retirement ended when a friend approached him with an interesting challenge and some serious cash. That lure proved irresistible. He didn't know how long he might be retired this time. But, meanwhile, he was staying busy in his business of fabricating window shutters. Of course, he didn't install them himself anymore, unless he just felt like it; somebody else now did that. In addition, he had some rental property halfway across the country that he maintained.

Unfortunately, he had to return to Florida in a couple of days because his wife had to go to work. She works only two days a week, which is just enough so she can keep her health insurance. She intends to continue part-time until she can quit 18 months shy of her 65th birthday. Then she will continue making payments on her health insurance under COBRA until she becomes eligible for Medicare.

Although there are plenty of folks who get their gold watch, cash in their 401(k), hit the ground running, and never look back, Walter represents a new face of retirement. In his 70s, he isn't sitting on the porch, rocking occasionally, staring out into the distance, sipping lemonade, and waiting to die. He's healthy, vigorous, happy, and fully engaged. He's in and out of the workforce as often as the spirit moves him.

Walter is fortunate. For him, work is optional. He certainly isn't starving, but money still motivated him when a new opportunity came up. Even his current situation is hardly the traditional definition of retirement. Although he's spending a fair amount of time cruising the water, maintaining rental properties and running a fabrication business isn't exactly fully retired. For folks like Walter, retirement is a state of mind.

In another important respect, this story is all too typical. Health-cost concerns are the black cloud hanging over all but the richest retirees. Many people feel forced to keep working because there isn't a realistic substitute for employer-supplied health insurance until you are eligible for Medicare. At that, not all health insurance is very good.

The single largest cause of bankruptcy is not credit card abuse, but medical disaster, affecting about two million American families each year—many of them middle class, and many of them with health coverage.[1]

---

[1] Himmelstein, David U., et al., "MarketWatch: Illness and Injury as Contributors to Bankruptcy," *Health Affairs*, Feb. 2, 2005, http://content.healthaffairs.org/cgi/content/abstract/hlthaff.w5.63.

In many couples, somebody has to work until the last of them is eligible for Medicare. The retirement of the bread earners alone doesn't suffice to cover their dependents. Of course, Medicare by itself leaves huge holes in our medical coverage. And it's almost impossible to estimate what they might be for an individual retiree or couple.

Absent radical health care reform, the situation will get progressively worse. America can't come close to funding the promises Medicare has made to the American public—and those promises are pretty shabby. They don't begin to solve the retiree's problem. If you think Social Security is a looming problem, wait until the bills for Medicare come rolling into the government. You haven't seen anything yet!

And don't even think that Medicare will cover the cost of long-term health care. It won't. Private long-term care insurance is expensive, reflecting both the high chance that an aging population will need help at some point in their lives and the ever-escalating $100,000 annual cost of care in many communities. A comprehensive plan for a single 60-year-old can easily reach a $5,000 a year premium. So, the retiree either bears a heavy lifetime load of insurance premiums, or runs the risk of potentially catastrophic long-term care costs.

In my parents' time, not many people lived to 70 and, of those who did, few were healthy enough to work. Today, people live a lot longer, and many of them enjoy good health late into their lives. That's another facet of the new retirement landscape. Many seniors can work longer, and many want to work longer, even if they don't have to.

Seniors may be in great demand as the workforce dries up at the younger ages. Like that of many mature industrialized countries, the U.S. birth rate is falling. Either our workers will have to work longer, or the shortfall will have to be covered by immigration. There is a shift in attitude about senior workers. Instead of being considered obsolete old fogies, they are being sought out for their experience, maturity, work ethic, judgment, and knowledge. There are many people who have retired or were downsized one week and then were hired back in the same position as "consultants"—some at increases in compensation— the following week. Indeed, many others are enjoying their second or third careers in entirely unrelated fields.

Some forward-thinking human relations consultants are already beginning to consider what kind of adaptations companies are going to require in order to induce senior managers and skilled workers to stay in the workforce as the supply of experienced employees dries up. The boomers may demand and get major concessions to tempt them off the golf courses. Reduced work weeks, flex time, telecommuting, additional vacations, expanded health benefits, reduced responsibilities with lower stress, and sabbaticals are all being studied as means to keep the workforce staffed and humming. But this, in turn, may set off additional inter-generational tensions as younger workers perceive this as preferential treatment.

That's the good news. But, there is another side. Longer life means more capital required to support your needs. One definition of retirement is that it is over one-third of your life without a paycheck. Even if you have adequate capital at the commencement of retirement, the margin of error for investment mistakes shrinks to almost nothing. You have got to get it right the first time, and you have to tend your nest egg continuously.

Demand for experienced senior workers is good news for those who are healthy, but unfortunately not every senior is able to work. Health is a wild card where we are all one stroke, heart attack, or kidney failure from forced retirement. Available good jobs and a financial need to work don't mean that each of us will be able to work.

Not every senior in the workforce is there voluntarily. Some are there because they lack the financial resources to retire. For them, work is mandatory. If you are lucky, you can continue with your job or transfer into another with similar compensation. But, if you lack the specific set of skills that our rapidly changing economy demands, your prospects for continued employment may be bleak. Not every greeter at Wal-Mart is there because they're lonely or bored.

Work Optional

So, the new retirement doesn't have a single face or dimension. It's as individual as you are. The one common thread is that all of us would like to reach a point where work is optional.

When work is optional, it takes on a whole new character. It's a liberating feeling to know that you can pack it in if you desire, change careers, or go to work as long as it's fun and rewarding. When you reach the point where you can tell the boss to "take this job and shove it," you may very well find that you don't want to.

Work is optional when you have built up sufficient capital to sustain yourself indefinitely and employ it effectively enough to reliably generate the income you need to support your desired lifestyle.

You will probably agree that the goal of making work optional and providing economic security, rather than retreating to the front porch hammock, far better meets the needs of today's worker. With adequate economic resources and simple advanced planning, retirement can really be the golden years. Or, retirement age may be the most fun you ever had at work.

Unfortunately, you are in the ocean, whether you like it or not. This book can show you how to swim, but only you can do it. Sink or swim, it's your choice.

Lesson 3

The Retirement Problem

It's expensive to retire. It's going to take a lot of capital assets—money that must be put to work—to replace your income. After all, one definition of retirement is that it is one-third of your life without a paycheck. You have to plan to live on your accumulated capital for more than 40 years.

Do-It-Yourself

www.Sink-Swim.com

Life Expectancy: This calculator can give you an idea of your life expectancy based on your current age, smoking habits, gender, and several other important lifestyle choices.

The retirement problem is simple: Create enough capital over your working career to support you comfortably for the rest of your life. Then make sure that capital lasts forever, or at least as long as you do.

Do-It-Yourself

www.Sink-Swim.com

Retirement Nest Egg Calculator: Do you know how much it takes to create a secure retirement? Use this calculator to help determine what size your retirement nest egg should be.

Do-It-Yourself

www.Sink-Swim.com

Investment Distributions: This calculator helps you determine either how long or how much periodic distributions can be taken out of an investment before it runs out.

What you should do today depends on what type of lifestyle you want at retirement, where you are in your career, what types of pension plans you have, and how much you have already accumulated.

It's not that difficult. Here's what you have to do:

- Put your savings on autopilot at a high level. Save first!
- Invest smart. Diversify globally. Control risk, cost, and taxes.
- Adopt a "Glide Slope" asset allocation policy so you are always taking just the appropriate amount of risk. The Glide Slope approach, explained later in the book, systematically reduces your equity exposure as you near your target retirement date.
- If you have a quality pension, use it effectively. If not, know your alternatives.

Time is your most valuable commodity when you accumulate and your enemy when you start to take withdrawals. So, let's get started. There is not a second to waste.

Please check www.Sink-Swim.com for calculators, updates, and additional information, such as articles and links to valuable outside resources. Also, read the Sink or Swim blog and join in the discussion group.

Part II

MEET YOUR
RETIREMENT PLANS

Lesson 4

Defined Benefit Plans

In this lesson, you learn the good, the bad, and the ugly about your pension plans, and how to maximize your benefits under your employer's plans.

Pension Plans

Because you are going to be responsible for your own retirement in a sink or swim environment, you need to understand your pension plan. This means knowing how to calculate benefits, what happens if the plan fails, and how to maximize your own benefits under the plan.

At their best, pension plans offer automatic savings, economical and effective investment options, and tax deferral. A good pension can be a great way to accumulate toward your goal. Not everyone has a high-quality pension plan available to them, however. Not all pensions are created equal. So, you need to know how yours works and if you should contribute to it.

The following sections explain how each of the major types of plans work. You can safely skip the plans that your employer isn't offering.

Defined Benefit Plans

The traditional American defined benefit (DB) retirement plan enables you to sit down with a calculator and DB plan documents to determine exactly what your benefit will be at retirement age. A DB plan provides a safe, predictable income stream for the balance of a retiree's life and for the retiree's survivor.

As the name implies, in a DB plan, you know the benefit, but not the cost to provide it. But, as employees, we don't care. It's somebody else's problem.

All the funding requirements, the investment policy decisions, the actual investment results, and the administrative costs are the responsibility of the employer or plan sponsor. If all goes well, from the employee viewpoint, the plan is on autopilot and they're along for the ride. The employee makes no decisions, has no responsibilities, seldom contributes a single penny, can count on a known retirement income, and has no worries.

The employer has almost the opposite perspective. Employers are solely responsible for the operation, cost, administration, and success of the plan. Worse yet, funding requirements cannot be determined accurately in advance. Plan under-funding shows up as a balance sheet liability, which can rapidly destroy shareholder equity and torpedo stock prices. During the stock market downturns of 2000 to 2002, several giant, household-name companies had unfunded liabilities far in excess of their net worth.

In theory, pension fund liability has a very high priority in the event of plan termination or corporate bankruptcy. The plan stands close to the head of the line when it comes time to divvy up remaining corporate assets. However, in practice, many companies just dump the entire mess into the hands of the Pension Benefit Guarantee Corporation (a government-funded insurance company that protects defined benefit pensions) and then bargain away any liability as part of their emergence from bankruptcy.

DB plans are very expensive to run. Because funding adequacy is so difficult to determine, the plans must have an annual actuarial certification. Additionally, after many high-profile plan failures, the 1974 Employee Retirement Income Security Act (ERISA) requires most plans to pay an annual per-participant insurance fee to the Pension Benefit Guarantee Corporation (PBGC) to guarantee partial benefits under the plan. (Small company plans sponsored by professional corporations and owner-only plans might be exempt.)

The inability to forecast accurately annual costs and the exposure to potential for liability swings due to outside influences (the stock markets) beyond the control of the company have forced many companies to abandon DB plans entirely. Although not extinct, DB plans are a shrinking part of the retirement landscape.

Like all other qualified pension plans, there is an initial employment period before an employee joins the plan. After that, the employee earns benefits according to the plan formula. But those benefits may vest over time. That means that if employees don't stick around for the required vesting period, they may forfeit all or a part of their accrued benefits. After the vesting period, employees are vested in all past and future benefits they accrue. Participation requirements and vesting periods serve to reduce costs for short-term employees, making it possible for employers to reward their most loyal long-term employees.

A typical benefit formula might look something like this: retirement income payable at age 65 = (2% for each year of service) × (the average gross pay for the last five years of employment pay).

For instance, an employee with 20 years of service whose average pay for the last five years was $50,000 would receive $20,000 annually: 20 years × 2% per year × $50,000 = $20,000 per year pension.

This basic benefit may then be adjusted for early or late retirement, and then further adjusted for the form of annuity selected by the retiree. This type of formula strongly favors older employees and employees with long service. Older employees who join the plan have fewer years until their benefits must be funded, so it takes proportionally more to fund their benefits than for younger employees. The formula is often referred to as "back-end loaded" because most of the benefits accrue during the last few years of service. Two factors of the formula—final average pay and years of service—both increase with longevity. As a result, most employees who don't stay with one company for an entire career end up with only a collection of token benefits.

These token benefits are generally not "portable," which means that they can't be rolled over into an IRA or the next corporate plan to grow for the future. They are typically "frozen" in the former employer's plan until the normal retirement date. This feature may not be an optimal arrangement for today's mobile employees.

Although the benefit formula imagines a level payment to a single retired person for life, that's not the usual outcome. ERISA requires that a married participant's default option is a Joint and One Half Annuity. This means that a lesser benefit is paid to retirees for the balance of their lives in order to provide for a death benefit to a surviving spouse of one half the remaining amount. For instance, retirees who had a nominal benefit of $50,000 a year might find that their Joint and One Half annuity benefit was $40,000 in order to ensure that if they died before their spouse, the spouse would receive a benefit of $20,000 for the balance of their life. To protect the spouse, this benefit arrangement can be waived only with the written and notarized consent of the spouse.

 Do-It-Yourself

www.Sink-Swim.com

Pension Plan Retirement Options: Use this calculator to help decide between joint survivorship and single survivorship pension options.

Some plans allow the retiring employee to elect a lump-sum settlement in lieu of a lifetime annuity. The amount of the lump sum is the calculated cost of providing the single life annuity, or buying one from an insurance company. This calculation is very sensitive to the assumed interest rate on the day of retirement. So, to maximize their lump-sum payment, employees may attempt to retire when they think interest rates are at a historical low point. In extreme cases, where many employees attempt to bail out at the same time, the large lump-sum payments can weaken the funding for remaining employees.

Unlike their defined contribution cousins, DB plans do not segregate assets for each employee. Employees cannot look at their account to see what the balance is. Instead, the plan has a single pooled account to satisfy all the expected liabilities. The employee should receive an annual statement called a Summary Annual Report that details the plan's financial condition and annual benefit statement. The annual benefit statement discloses the employee's accrued benefits, and the Summary Annual Report should show the status of the plan's funding.

In reality, most plans are under-funded if for no other reason than the difficulty of estimating future benefit levels. How could a company accurately estimate 20 or 30 years in advance what an employee's final five years' average pay might be? It's an ever-changing, exponentially growing target. Reasonable amounts of under-funding are not generally critical problems for a healthy company because the company is allowed to amortize the under-funding over many future years. Additionally, companies are allowed some leeway to "normalize" funding by over-contributing or under-contributing to the estimated target contribution level depending on their annual financial results. However, a chronically weak company that has a severely under-funded plan is a ticket for disaster for both employee and employer.

Although a guaranteed income for life with no investment responsibilities or risk sounds pretty nice, there is a dark side: If things go wrong, it can get awful very quickly. Your plan may be frozen, terminated, or terminated in distress. None of that is good for you, especially if you are late in your career.

The maximum benefit in 2008 that a qualified DB plan can fund toward is 100% of compensation, or $185,000 per year, whichever is smaller at normal retirement age. There are a variety of additional regulations designed to prevent the plan design from blatantly discriminating in favor of highly compensated employees.

Lesson 5

Defined Contribution Plans—An Overview

Like it or not, defined contribution (DC) plans are the wave of the future. Understanding how they work, and how to make them work to meet your needs, is a critical part of your retirement strategy.

DC pension plans come in several flavors, each with their own particular quirks. They all share common traits: A formula determines how much is contributed for each participant, and each participant has a separate account or readily identified share of a pooled account. The ultimate benefit depends on the investment results of the account.

This design concept has important implications for both plan sponsors and participants.

For Plan Sponsors

Most importantly, because there is no fixed retirement benefit guarantee, the problem of under-funding that was so vexing in the defined benefit pension plan is not an issue. After the plan contribution is made, the sponsor need not be concerned about potential future pension liabilities. There is no possibility that a down securities market can destroy earnings or decimate the balance sheet.

The sponsor can budget annual costs with a great deal of certainty:

- Plan administration, compliance, and associated costs can be substantially reduced. There is no annual actuarial reporting and no PBGC insurance requirement.
- Plan administration and investment costs can be shifted entirely to the participants if the sponsor so elects.
- In plans that allow self-direction *and* that comply with certain "safe harbor" provisions, fiduciary liability for investment choices can be substantially eliminated.
- A portion or all of the funding costs might be shifted to the participants through required contributions, matching requirements, or pre-tax contributions.

For Participants

From the participant's point of view, some benefits are problematic; some are not. Each advantage to the employer, however, usually comes at a cost to the employee:

- Accurate forecasting of benefits is not possible.
- The plans tend to be more "portable" when changing jobs.
- Younger participants have proportionally more benefit per dollar spent on the plan at retirement than older participants.
- Especially for younger participants, with decent investment results, there is a possibility for higher benefits than a defined benefit might offer.
- If plans feature self-direction, the entire responsibility for investment outcome shifts to employees. Investment choices available under the plan may be inadequate to properly control risk and reward characteristics of the account.
- Where administrative and investment costs are passed on to the employee, they may be so burdensome that they substantially reduce future benefits.
- Where contributions by employees are required, employees must determine if the benefits provided by the plan are superior to their other alternatives.

Lesson 6

The Basic Defined Contribution Plan

The "vanilla" DC plan is also called a Money Purchase Pension Plan (MPPP). The plan sponsor simply contributes to an account according to a formula, usually based on compensation. The account grows until the employee either terminates or retires. Then, the vested balance is turned over to the employee, often as a lump sum or, alternatively and less frequently, as an annuity. This type of design clearly benefits younger employees who have a long time for the account to grow before it is needed.

Defined contribution plans offer a powerful combination of benefits to both sponsor and participant, as follows:

- The contribution is fully tax-deductible for the sponsor, and not taxable for the employee. The employee even escapes Social Security and Medicare tax on the contribution.
- Contributions grow free of tax burden until distributed. While the funds are inside the plan, there is no tax drag for dividends, capital gains, or interest.
- Participants may be in a lower bracket when funds are distributed than during their working career. Deductions at a high marginal tax rate coupled with distributions at a lower tax rate are a powerful leverage of the tax system.
- Assuming the sponsor makes the contributions in a timely manner, the fund can never be under-funded.
- The funds are in a separate trust for the benefit of the employees/participants. Even if the sponsor company vaporizes, the trust is protected against creditors.
- Savings are automatic because the funds never reach the employee and go directly to a retirement investment program.

In 2008, the maximum contribution per individual is $46,000 or 25% of compensation, whichever is less. Limits increase $2,000 a year through 2010.

Here's an example of how this simplest of DC plans might work:

> The company contributes 10% of compensation to a pension fund each year. Two employees each make $50,000 a year. The company contributes $5,000 for each. One employee enters the plan at age 25, and the other at age 45. Assuming they both work until age 65 and that the plan has a compound return of 8% per year, the younger employee can look forward to a benefit of $1,295,282, while the older receives only $228,809. The difference in benefit ($1,066,472) has little to do with what the company contributed (in this case, an additional $100,000) and a lot to do with the additional time the money had to grow.

---

www.Sink-Swim.com   # Do-It-Yourself

Retirement Pension Planner: Plan your retirement with a company pension, find out if you are on track, and learn how to stay there.

Retirement Planner: Quickly determine if your retirement plan is on track—and learn how to keep it there.

Retirement Shortfall: Running out of your retirement savings too soon is one of the biggest risks to a comfortable retirement. Use this calculator to find a potential shortfall in your current retirement savings plan.

Another big factor that impacts the final benefit is the plan's investment return. If the plan's net return in our previous example increased to 9%, the final lump sums rise to $1,689,412 and $255,800, respectively. These are significant differences, at least in my neighborhood. So, actual plan earnings are critical to a secure retirement for the participant.

Do-It-Yourself

www.Sink-Swim.com

Compare Savings Rates: Even a small difference in the interest you are paid on your savings can add up over time. Use this calculator to see how different savings rates can impact your savings strategy!

Mutual Fund Expense Calculator: This calculator can help you analyze the costs associated with buying shares in a mutual fund. By entering a few pieces of information, found in your fund's prospectus, you can see the impact of fees and operating expenses on your investment.

Investment Returns: Use this calculator to help you see how inflation, taxes, and your time horizon can impact your bottom line. There is more to investing than knowing your annual rate of return.

In a DB plan, the plan sponsor must make up any deficiency if investment returns fall below target. This is not the case in a DC plan. There is no target accumulation, and poor returns simply result in low benefits. However, as fiduciaries, plan sponsors must ensure that the plan assets are invested prudently. The record is decidedly mixed.

Plan sponsors should not invest in just any old junk. ERISA dictates very stringent fiduciary obligations that have been further expanded by a Uniform State Prudent Investor Act, a mountain of case law, and volumes of regulations. Together, they set a very high standard for anyone who has responsibility over investment decisions for qualified plans. Additionally, ERISA and subsequent regulations impose personal liability for breaches of fiduciary duties by plan sponsors, investment advisors, investment committees, investment managers, and all other people charged with plan supervision.

Plan sponsors can and should delegate some of their responsibilities to a "prudent expert." However, they must carefully select and continuously monitor the advisor, and they can never completely escape their obligations or liability.

Investment Control and Safe Harbor Provisions

If the plan sponsor retains investment control by offering no investment options to employees, it also retains fiduciary liability for the investment results. Participants may later claim that the plan was too risky, causing them loss, or that the plan was so conservative that they didn't obtain market returns.

As you can imagine, many plan fiduciaries do not enthusiastically embrace any form of liability that they might be able to unload. As it turns out, they can shed a great deal of it—but not nearly as much as many of them might think. ERISA contains "safe harbor" provisions that, if met, transfer much of the investment risk to the plan participant. By offering participants a choice of investment options in a form that complies with the ERISA regulations, liability for the investment results is transferred to the participant. The so-called Section 404(c) provisions are almost universally misunderstood and far too often misapplied with unfortunate results for the participants.

Although often displayed by glib salespeople on a single slide with four bullet points, the actual subsection is 12 single-spaced pages covering 74 distinct points in the code and requires far more than most plans offer. Failure to comply fully with the provisions extinguishes the safe harbor hopes of the plan sponsors. Worse yet, it limits the ability of participants to control their investment results, optimize returns, and limit risk.

Funding Options

Participants might be offered insurance company separate accounts, mutual funds, co-mingled trusts, or other pooled investments to choose from. In most cases, the plan offers from 6 to 100 funds with differing investment objectives.

In DB plans, the sponsor contributes both investment funding plus plan administration costs. In DC plans, the sponsor can either pay the administration costs separately as a necessary and proper business expense, or have them deducted from the participant accounts. The second option shifts the cost to the participant, and reduces the ultimate benefit proportionately.

Portability

DC plans are usually much more portable than DB plans. Participants are encouraged to take their pension balances with them when they change employers. This opens up opportunities for the knowledgeable or pitfalls for the unwary. A subsequent chapter explores the options for employees changing jobs.

Lesson 7————————————

Profit-Sharing Plans

Profit-sharing plans are a type of defined contribution plan almost identical to Money Purchase Pension Plans (MPPP), except that the sponsor is not required to make a fixed annual contribution. In a good year, they can increase contributions, and in a bad year, they can reduce or suspend them. This kind of flexibility is important to many businesses. It encourages companies that otherwise might be reluctant to assume a fixed regular contribution formula to start and maintain plans.

Profit-sharing contributions can create and maintain morale by rewarding the entire employee group for productivity gains, cost savings initiatives, or meeting other corporate goals. Properly employed, they can be a powerful incentive by giving employees an ownership-like stake in the success of the enterprise.

From the employee's side, it's more difficult to forecast retirement benefits or determine funding needs where the employer has a lower commitment to annual funding, or varies the funding on a year-to-year basis.

Lesson 8

Employee-Funded Plans

With a Money Purchase Pension Plan or a profit-sharing plan, the employer makes all the contributions. All eligible employees receive a benefit.

On the other hand, 401(k), 403(b), and 457 plans are funded by employees out of their earnings. Participation is voluntary. Employees are free to contribute or not as they see fit.

A huge common problem with all employee-funded plans is that although employees bear the cost, they have almost no control over the quality of the plan. They must simply take what they are given and try to make the most of it. Too often, what they are given is disgracefully bad.

Employers are either indifferent or inept in selection of plan providers. They focus on features rather than results. Web sites, technology, and other bright shiny objects are no substitute for economical and effective investment plans.

They rely on big, brand-name providers and focus on ease of administration for the employer rather than plan costs and effectiveness of investment options for the employee.

If employees opt out, they give up the tax-favored treatment, asset protection, and systematic investments that qualified plans offer. In many cases, they can do as well or better on the outside by funding an IRA; however, for highly compensated employees, this may not be possible because the $5,000 IRA limit may not be as much as they need to put away.

Lesson 9 ———————————————————

Generic Problems with Pension Plans

What Is Wrong with Self-Funded, Self-Directed Plans?

When it was first introduced, the 401(k) plan was not intended to be a replacement for the traditional pension—it was designed to supplement the traditional plan. Today, the 401(k) is fast replacing the traditional plan.

From the employee's perspective, it offers far less in guaranteed benefits, and shifts much of the burden for providing a decent retirement to the employee. Let's take a look at what we have lost, and how the 401(k) compares.

As the nation's primary pension system, the 401(k) leaves a lot to be desired. Far too many employees underutilize the system, fail to participate, make inappropriate investment choices, borrow too much of their account balances, and withdraw their balances from the system when changing jobs.

As a review, under a traditional plan, employees need only to show up for work reliably enough to keep their jobs, thus earning a guaranteed retirement income for life. Using a simple formula based on years of service and earnings, employees could forecast their retirement income to the penny and rely on it arriving each month for as long as they lived.

Simply put, the employer did it all. No more! A 401(k) shifts almost all this responsibility to the worker. The message couldn't be much clearer: "Sink or swim; we don't care."

If you are a libertarian, you might advance the argument that you have empowered the worker. Of course, nobody asked the workers if they prefer to go it alone. Why would they ever want to?

Unfortunately, there is precious little evidence that the vast majority of American workers are ready, willing, or able to assume these responsibilities. Sure, there are exceptions, but they are far from the rule.

Few employees combine the talents of certified actuaries, investment advisors, and life insurance agents, which would be necessary to do the job properly. Why should they? They practice medicine, fix automobiles, write advertising, or any of the other thousands of occupations that make an economy hum.

Few employees are inclined to take the time to establish financial goals, define investment policy, conduct annual reviews, purchase insurance, re-allocate their assets, or check out new investment options. We are all time-stressed. My "To Do" list grows by the day.

Few people have the inclination, discipline, or financial ability to save adequate amounts to meet reasonable goals. They are barraged all day, every day, with the message to spend, spend, spend!

The overwhelming evidence tells us that across the entire block of plans, it's not working.

Endless studies confirm that participants do the following:

- Make irrational asset allocation choices
- Decline to participate when eligible
- Leave funds indefinitely in cash
- Neglect to re-allocate or rebalance
- Fail to adjust asset allocation to meet lifecycle needs
- Borrow out funds from accounts
- Cannot estimate retirement needs

- Fail to accumulate sufficient funds to support their perceived needs at retirement
- Are unsure how to convert a lump sum into a lifetime income

Even if all participants made perfect decisions, they are often stuck in plans that are sub-standard and dirt poor:

- Few plan sponsors understand or are concerned about fiduciary compliance.
- The consulting model is riddled with conflicts of interest.
- Bundled suppliers fail fully and fairly to disclose, instead willfully obscuring costs, conflicts of interest, or performance information.

Because the employee bears the entire burden of poor performance and high cost, employers feel little economic pressure to improve the plans.

The inevitable result is high-cost, high-risk, chronic poor performance, insufficient choices to allocate funds properly, and poor plan design. Some plans are so horrible that employees should rightfully opt out. Unfortunately, they may not be able to put as much away in an IRA, or due to income limitations, they may not be able to have an IRA at all. Employers offering such shoddy plans should be ashamed, but are generally clueless.

Although 401(k) plans are generally much more "portable" than defined benefit plans, vesting requirements and elimination periods slash potential benefits for job switchers. In some cases, people switching jobs may lose up to two years of eligibility to participate because under their old employer's plan, they must be employed on the last day of the plan year, and under the new plan, they must have been employed for a period of time before they are eligible. Given that the average length of employment is now under 4½ years, an employee could lose many years in the system if they job hop. And not all job changes are voluntary. Workers often find that they are furloughed, terminated, downsized, outsourced, or their employer fails entirely.

Additionally, there is an unfortunate tendency to cash out accounts when changing jobs—in spite of daunting tax penalties. Across the system, there is a huge "leakage" of assets as job-hopping employees finance cars or vacations rather than roll over their accounts. Additionally, some may be forced to tap into their accounts to bridge the gaps between jobs if unemployment doesn't provide sufficient assets and other savings are inadequate.

Highly compensated employees may not be able to contribute as much as they would like because rank-and-file workers won't contribute at all or contribute very little. Under arcane "testing" requirements, the highly compensated individuals' contributions are limited if the rank–and-file contributions fall below certain thresholds.

At the other end of the scale, minimum wage employees may feel hard pressed to finance their retirement out of their meager wages and be able to eat, too.

The Pension Protection Act (PPA) of 2006 made some improvements in 401(k)s. By encouraging automatic enrollment, providing for default investment other than cash, and for automatic escalation of contributions over time, the act allowed plans to "nudge" employees in the right direction. However, the employee always has the ability to "opt out" of the plan.

Additionally, the PPA allows for "fiduciary advisors" to give individually tailored advice to plan participants. However, if the fiduciary advisor is simply in the position of choosing the least awful choices available under the plan, that's not too helpful. And another layer of fees and expenses born by the employee further reduces the future benefits for participants. As of this writing, the Labor Department has not issued regulations that spell out how such advice must be given.

Investor Behavior

Economists have long wondered why investors get such dismal results and how they make economic decisions. Evidently, investors aren't the rational critters that economic theory suggests they are. Behavioral finance examines how what investors do influences the result that they get. It's a serious, fascinating subject, combining psychology, economics, and game theory. What they have learned about us isn't very flattering. As a group, we investors look like we are hard-wired for failure.

Of course, there are always exceptions, but across the masses, the investor gets a small fraction of what the market delivers. How can that be in an efficient market? Investors ought to expect market returns plus or minus a little random error. But, they get far, far less.

It turns out that even though markets are highly efficient, investors are highly inefficient. By far the biggest risk investors face is their own behavior. Investors systematically shoot themselves in the foot. Many people are financially illiterate, yet at the same time, grossly overconfident of their skills. Investors don't all make the same mistakes at once, but most fall prey to one or more of a highly predictable series of mistakes, which we call the seven deadly sins of portfolio management, as follows:

1. Investors chase performance. This is an inspired way to destroy your portfolio. One of the very few things that Wall Street tells you that you can take to the bank is that past returns are not an indication of future returns. Someone is always going to beat the market. But, it's most likely that they did so through pure dumb luck, or worse yet, by taking excessive risks. Excess returns generate huge amounts of cash flow for an investment manager, fattening their bonuses and providing an incentive to violate the normal rules of prudence. For the investor, chasing those "hot" managers with their juicy returns leads to an endless cycle of buying high, selling low, and wondering why you are not making money in the capital markets.

2. You buy costly investments. If you want exposure to domestic large company stocks, you can buy the Vanguard S&P 500 with no commission (sales load), no 12(b)-1 fee (distribution expense allowance), no revenue sharing, and a total expense ratio of 0.18 percent. Or you can pay several percent in commission on your purchase and then spend close to 3% a year for a managed account, mutual fund, annuity product, or variable life insurance products. Those additional costs come right out of your returns. You are as likely to garner additional returns over and above the additional expenses as you are to see pigs fly. The most likely case is that you will under-perform the market by the amount of your additional expenses while bearing higher risk.

Do-It-Yourself

www.Sink-Swim.com

Compare Investment Fees: You will find that even a small difference in the fees you pay on your investments can add up over time. Use this calculator to see how different fees impact your investment strategy!

---

3. You buy investments with high turnover, or they endlessly trade their own accounts. Day trading is not the road to riches. The more you trade, the lower your returns. It's highly unlikely that you can "beat the market" with your inspired trading. Trading has direct and indirect costs that reliably reduce returns. It won't matter whether you do it, or your manager does it for you. High trading reduces average returns.

Do-It-Yourself

www.Sink-Swim.com

Compare Savings Rates: Even a small difference in the interest you are paid on your savings can add up over time. Use this calculator to see how different savings rates can impact your savings strategy!

4. Many investors fail to match their portfolio to their risk tolerance, time horizon, and objectives. If you don't take sufficient risk, you will never obtain any reasonable objectives. If you take too much risk, your portfolio may implode. The amount of risk should be varied with your financial circumstances to match your unique requirements.

Do-It-Yourself

www.Sink-Swim.com

Asset Allocator: Your age, ability to tolerate risk, and several other factors are used to calculate a desirable mix of stocks, bonds, and cash.

---

5. Few investors properly diversify their investments. The portfolio with the highest return per unit of risk is globally diversified. The further you get from a properly diversified portfolio, the higher your risk and the lower your probability of success. This is discussed in more detail later.

6. You attempt to time the market swings and let emotions, hunches, media coverage, and cocktail party chat drive you in and out of the market at just the wrong times.

7. You don't provide enough liquidity to meet known cash flow needs, or ride out a down market.

Do-It-Yourself

www.Sink-Swim.com

Emergency Savings Calculator: This calculator helps you determine how much emergency savings you may need, and how you can begin saving toward this important goal.

Other mental roadblocks that can lead you to inappropriate decision making include the following:

- **Loss aversion.** You are so loss averse that, psychologically, you weigh losses twice as heavily as gains.
- **Heuristics.** You use unsuitable mental shortcuts (oversimplification) when faced with complex decisions.
- **You are otherwise human.** You procrastinate, make inconsistent choices, mentally heavily discount your future needs, fail to follow through on positive resolutions, and frame problems too narrowly.

The problems Americans face are the same inside their pensions as for their personal investments. You have to get a grip on your own behavior and cure your bad habits before you can be effective investors.

You don't have to be a victim. As an individual, you may or may not have some of these behavioral problems. Very simple planning that incorporates basic financial theory combined with a little old-fashioned discipline can prevent all of these foibles.

If you recognize some of your less-than-helpful habits, you can break them. Later, you see how to create highly effective portfolios that are low cost, low risk, and low tax exposure.

If you can't or won't spend the time to do it yourself, seek a professional advisor's help!

Of course, finding the right advisor requires proper consideration. Otherwise, you can jump right out of the frying pan into the fire. Brokers may be just as prone to bad behavior as their clients. One recent major study indicates that broker-advised clients do relatively worse in all investment types than self-directed clients. In other words, for a variety of reasons, the value of a stockbroker's advice may be far less than zero!

Lesson 10

The 401(k) Plan

As previously mentioned, when 401(k) plans were first conceived, they were intended to be a supplement to traditional plans, not a replacement. Ted Benna, a benefits consultant, designed a plan to allow some employees of a small bank to tax shelter a bonus if they so desired, while allowing other employees to take the bonus in cash. (The bank president wanted to defer his bonus, but felt that most of the rank-and-file would prefer cash.) The rest is history. The idea took off, grabbing an increasing share of the total retirement plan landscape.

As a supplemental plan, the 401(k) plan is a truly great idea. As such, it is often offered in combination with other pension plans. A 401(k) plan gives employees an opportunity to defer income by making voluntary "pre-tax" contributions to a retirement account up to certain limits. The 2008 limits are $16,000, with an additional $5,000 catch-up contribution for participants over age 50. Both limits increase $500 a year until 2010. Employees are always fully vested in their own contributions, but are subject to vesting schedules on the employer's contributions, if any. Although contributions are pre-tax, or deferrals, they are subject to both Social Security and Medicare withholding. The combination of current tax deduction, tax-free accumulation inside the plan, and potentially lower taxes during retirement are a compelling advantage.

www.Sink-Swim.com

Do-It-Yourself

401(k) Savings Calculator: A 401(k) can be one of your best tools for creating a secure retirement. Use this calculator to see why this is a retirement savings plan you cannot afford to pass up.

401(k) Savings with Profit Sharing: Use this calculator to see how a 401(k) with profit-sharing plan can help you save for retirement.

Under various arcane "non-discrimination" and "top heavy" rules, if not enough of the lower-paid employees participate, then the higher-paid employees cannot contribute as much as they might like. To encourage sufficient participation, most plans offer an employer "match." Employees that make contributions will have some or all of their contributions matched by the employer. These matching contributions range from exceedingly generous to something even Scrooge would have been ashamed of. For instance, many plans call for the employer to put in 4% of compensation if the employee puts in 5%. But one plan the author came across in his practice called for the employer to contribute 1% if the employee contributed 10%.

Technically, the 401(k) is a profit-sharing plan with voluntary employee contributions or deferrals. Like other defined contribution plans, the majority of 401(k) plans are "self-directed" in that the employee chooses from a limited menu of investment choices offered under the plan.

Today, many firms offer only a 401(k) plan for retirement benefits. As a standalone plan, even with a generous match, it falls far short of a perfect retirement solution.

The standalone, employee-funded, self-directed 401(k) plan is the last step in a long progression that shifts responsibility for retirement from the employer to the employee:

- The employees fund the plan from their wages through contribution of either pre-tax or post-tax (Roth) dollars.
- The employees bear the entire investment risk.
- The employees must determine how much to fund for retirement.
- The employees may (or may not) pay the entire cost of administration and investment management from their account balances.
- The employees must design their own asset allocation plan from the available choices within the plan.

The trend away from guaranteed secure retirements (DB) to a system where nobody cares if the employee sinks or swims (401[k]) is accelerating. If every employee was a disciplined, rational, investment professional, and if every plan offered the best possible investment choices, the system might work tolerably well. Here's a hint: The system looks like it's designed from the ground up for failure.

Lesson 11

The 403(b) Plan— Not-For-Profit Enterprises

Special plans for employees of non-profit institutions are called 403(b) plans. They are a close relative of the better-known 401(k) plan, but with a few interesting twists. These plans are available to public schools, hospitals, public and private universities, churches, and other non-profit organizations qualified under 501(c)(3). Employer-sponsored 403(b) plans are funded with both employer contributions and employee salary tax-deductible contributions. Employer contribution plans (other than those maintained by governmental agencies) must meet the requirements of the Employee Retirement Income Security Act of 1974 (ERISA).

Do-It-Yourself

www.Sink-Swim.com

403(b) Savings Calculator: If you are an employee of a non-profit tax-exempt organization, a 403(b) can be one of your best tools for creating a secure retirement.

Unlike corporate retirement plans, the sponsor usually doesn't run the plan as a trust. Most institutions contract with multiple providers to offer 403(b) benefit choices to their employees. The employee selects from the employer's providers and chooses from the investment options offered by that provider. The employer then makes contributions to the provider on behalf of the employee. After that, the sponsor usually washes its hands of the whole deal.

For historical reasons, 403(b) plans are often called tax-sheltered annuities (TSA). This is very unfortunate because there is no requirement to fund a 403(b) plan with an annuity at all. Let's say that differently: There is no excuse to fund a 403(b) plan with an annuity! Any mutual fund family could qualify as an offering, and mutual funds would almost always be a far better choice. There is simply no conceivable reason to pay an additional cost for an insurance company's Mortality and Expense (M&E) charge inside a tax-qualified plan. M&E charges are in theory supposed to cover the cost of providing an annuity guarantee upon retirement. In practice, it's an additional layer of expense that provides no benefit other than the insurance company profit.

A few institutions offer outstanding programs. These employers have done their homework and selected very high-quality providers that offer low-cost funds, adequate investment choices to build a sophisticated asset allocation plan, superior service, and meaningful education for their employees. Not all employees are so fortunate, however.

At the low end, it gets pretty raunchy. Little thought and no objective standards are applied to the selection process for providers. After providers are selected by the sponsor, their commissioned salespeople emerge from under their rocks to enroll their unwitting victims. They swarm like vultures in hospitals, schools, and colleges, posing as professional retirement counselors. You know the rest of the story: The companies with the highest costs pay the highest commissions and attract the most ruthless vultures. Insurance company salespeople misrepresent annuities as the required product for the plan. Employees end up with high-cost, low-quality products that unfortunately come with the strong implied endorsement of their employers. Meanwhile, some of the best value products, like Vanguard Funds, cannot afford vultures to lounge around campus.

Where employers abdicate their responsibilities as fiduciaries and delegate education and enrollment to plan providers, results can be far from happy. Provider salespeople with severe conflicts of interest are turned loose on trusting employees with the implied endorsement of the employer. This is the functional equivalent of inviting the foxes to dine with the chickens.

Is Your 403(b) Plan Broken?

A broken plan has some or all of the following problems:

- High-commission, high-cost products. Many products commonly marketed to 403(b) plan participants have annual costs exceeding 3%. It is not at all unusual for employees to be told that only high commission annuities can fund their plans. Nothing could be farther from the truth. There is almost no rational justification for the use of so-called TSAs in a 403(b) plan. No-load mutual funds would far better serve the retirement needs of participants.
- Surrender fees and/or withdrawal restrictions that trap an employee who wants to switch to a lower-cost, more effective provider plan.
- Investment choices might be so limited that it is impossible to diversify the portfolio properly or integrate it with the employee's other assets and financial planning.
- Information and education is inadequate to assist employees in making informed choices.

Employees with substandard 403(b) plans have three options:

- If the plan offers multiple providers, they may be able to switch their accounts to a better provider.
- Like employees in private industry, they can petition their employers to provide better options and suppliers. Depending on the employer, this may or may not be successful.

- If employees change employers, they may transfer their assets to another 403(b) plan unless the current plan documents specifically prohibit it. Most plans do not. The vast majority of the time, employees would be best served to roll over their account balance to an IRA.

Teachers, doctors, nurses, pastors, and other workers for America's non-profit enterprises deserve the best retirement plans.

Improving a broken 403(b) plan can yield enormous benefits. For instance, assume an employee with a total $5,000 annual contribution over 30 years. If the employee were able to increase the rate of return by 2% by simply cutting administrative costs, the increase would be staggering. At 7% compound return, the total after 30 years would be $505,365.21. However, at 9%, the balance grows to $742,876.09, an increase of 47%.

Don't just accept the status quo. Investigate all your options. Let your employer know if you don't have a first-class plan.

403(b)

The 403(b) environment really needs an extreme makeover. Insurance companies have a real stranglehold on the school districts that provide these plans, and they use their marketing power to prevent low-cost mutual funds from being offered.

In large part, this is because these plans were traditionally known as tax-sheltered annuities (TSAs). Historically, participants were only permitted by the Internal Revenue Code to purchase annuities in these accounts. Even though the tax laws changed many years ago to allow teachers to purchase mutual funds, school districts have been very slow to change. As a result, many school districts continue to give teachers only the option of investing in high-cost annuities. According to www.403bwise.com—a reputable and helpful website devoted to raising awareness of the problems with 403(b) plans—as of 2006, close to 80% of the $652 billion dollars invested in the 403(b) was parked in annuity products. Of this amount, 34% was invested in variable annuity products.

Because teachers and hospital workers who invest in 403(b) plans are typically looking for long-term gains to supplement their retirement savings, it makes no sense to invest in high-cost investments. These costs will kill your returns over the long haul.

Many of my cases over the last few years have involved suing brokerage firms for selling unsuitable variable annuities to investors. I was appalled to learn a couple of years ago that my own mother, an elementary school teacher for the last 35 years, owns a variable annuity inside of her 403(b) account. This caused me to look a lot deeper into the issue, and what I found was outrageous. Not only did her school district not offer no-load mutual fund options, but the teacher's union she was a member of endorsed high-cost annuity products.

The National Education Association (NEA) collected nearly $50 million in royalties in 2004 on the sale of annuities, life insurance, and other financial products. In addition, the New York State United Teachers (NYSUT) has received as much as $3 million a year in secret payments from ING Group for encouraging its 525,000 members to invest in an annuity sold by the insurance company and took steps to conceal its financial arrangement with ING from its members. The New York State Attorney General's Office investigated the relationship between NYSUT and ING. The investigation revealed that a 403(b) plan, offered by ING and endorsed by NYSUT's Member Benefits unit, charged investors fees and expenses as high as 2.85% per year, while delivering only limited benefits!

—*Contributed by Jason Doss*

Lesson 12 ———————————————

The Roth 401(k), 403(b) Option

A new option enables participants to forgo the current tax deduction on their contributions in favor of totally tax-free distributions later. This is particularly attractive to employees who believe they will be in a higher tax bracket after retirement, or who are currently in a low bracket but expect their career income to rise. Strangely enough, although there is an income limit for Roth IRA contributions, there is no income limit for Roth 401(k) contributions.

---

www.Sink-Swim.com

Do-It-Yourself

Roth 401(k) or Traditional 401(k): Use this calculator to help determine if a traditional 401(k) or Roth 401(k) might be best for you.

Roth 401(k) vs. Traditional 401(k) and Your Paycheck: See how a traditional or Roth 401(k) might affect your take-home pay, as well as your retirement savings.

Although the Roth is an attractive option, you shouldn't get hung up on endlessly studying whether to contribute to a Roth or traditional 401(k). The differences in after-tax, disposable income later are not very significant for most employees. The most important issue is deciding to make a substantial contribution to a savings and investment plan. If tax rates don't change, the after-tax future value of your contributions will be exactly the same.

See the material on Roth and Regular in Lesson 15, "IRAs," for a comparison of the tax treatments and advantages of each.

Lesson 13

Section 457 Plans for Municipal and State Employees

Municipal and state employees enjoy yet another variation of the defined contribution plan. Section 457 plans, however, are a distinct breed of animal with individual quirks. Typically, there is no employer match or contribution—only voluntary employee tax-deductible contributions.

Do-It-Yourself

www.Sink-Swim.com

457 Savings Calculator: A 457 plan can be one of your best tools for creating a secure retirement. Use this calculator to see why this is a retirement savings plan you cannot afford to pass up.

Technically, in a non-qualified, tax-deferral program, contributions are limited to the lesser of 100% of compensation or $15,500 in 2008. After that, the amount is indexed for inflation. There are special catch-up provisions for 457 plans. After age 50, the catch-up amount is $5,000 in 2008, with the additional contribution maximum of $20,500.

So far, it looks like a 401(k) plan. But here are some major differences:

- If participants are also eligible for a 401(k) or other defined benefit plan, they are eligible to make the maximum contribution to both plans.

- For the last three years before retirement, the catch-up is twice the normal allowance, so the employee could contribute a total of $25,500 in 2008.

- Recent legislation allows for rollovers into IRAs upon termination of employment, or a rollover into another 457 plan if desired.

- These plans have another unique feature: There is no 10% early distribution penalty. This could be a very useful feature for employees who retire early to a second career and may need to draw on the funds at some point before age 59½. However, if the plan is rolled over into an IRA, it becomes subject to the early withdrawal penalty like any other IRA.

- Unlike 401(k) plans and other defined benefit plans, loans are not allowed. Hardship withdrawals are allowed, but they are subject to ordinary income tax.

- ERISA does not apply to 457 plans, depriving these employees of some federal regulatory standards and oversight enjoyed by other qualified plan participants. Fiduciary standards may be problematical in some localities, and participants should use some independent judgment before deciding to enroll. All local governments are not uniformly honest and/or competent. Enough said.

Note: There are two additional completely different Section 457 plans that are not discussed here. Some church or non-governmental 501(c)(3) organizations have non-qualified, deferred compensation plans for their employees. There also are special deferred compensation plans for highly compensated state and municipal employees. Unfortunately, all three plans are called Section 457 plans, causing more than a little confusion because they are not similar at all.

Lesson 14 ——————————

Making the Most of Your
401(k), 403(b), or 457 Plan

Choosing the Right Plan Options

Use the glide slope approach explained later in Lesson 39, "Taking the Right Amount of Risk," to elect the right ratio of stocks to bonds for your point in your career. The glide slope approach systematically reduces your equity exposure as you near your target retirement date. Try to come as close as you can to global diversification within the plan choices. If you have low-cost index funds available, use them as your first choice to represent the asset classes. If not, select the best available choices by evaluating cost, number of holdings, and degree that it represents a specific style class that you want to hold in your portfolio. Very often, there are several good choices amid a sea of mediocre ones. Use them and build the rest of your portfolio elsewhere. If none of them are economical and effective, or if total plan costs are too high, don't contribute to the plan.

If you are fortunate in having a good plan, you can do all of your retirement savings and investment inside of it. Try to put away at least 15 percent of your pre-tax salary, and more if you started late.

If your plan has an automatic rebalancing feature, use it. Many plans require the participant to select rebalancing affirmatively. If your plan doesn't offer rebalancing, then make a point of rebalancing once a year. Otherwise, over time, your plan will grow so far out of balance that you won't recognize it.

Integrating Your Retirement Plan Assets into Your Total Financial Plan

Look at your entire family assets to develop an appropriate asset allocation and investment policy. The fact is you can't isolate retirement planning from all the other things going on in your life. You will have other concerns that must be accounted for, ranging from home purchase to college planning. These other objectives must be funded outside of your retirement plan. For instance, it won't do your child much good at college time if all your funds are locked up tight inside a retirement plan.

A single comprehensive investment plan that considers all your assets and all your goals will enable you to manage your financial future more effectively than if you try to have a separate plan for each objective. If you are working with a good investment advisor, the advisor will be able to integrate all your assets and objectives.

Lesson 15————————————

IRAs

Learning to Love IRAs

IRAs don't get enough respect. They are an extremely powerful wealth accumulation vehicle for individuals or families. In some very fundamental ways, they are the best and most flexible retirement plans. Americans should use them more.

Technically, IRAs are not a "qualified plan," so they are treated somewhat differently than corporate or non-profit plans. That's not all bad, but you need to understand the subtle differences.

As you see in the following list, the vast majority of American families can and should have IRAs. If you start early and invest wisely, they provide very substantial benefits:

Do-It-Yourself

www.Sink-Swim.com

Traditional IRA Calculator: How can contributing to a regular IRA help you in your retirement?

- You have complete control of the investment policy and costs associated with the plan. You can build a more effective, lower-cost retirement portfolio than available in 90% of the corporate or non-profit plans in this country.

- There is never a waiting period or "elimination period" before you qualify for contributions.
- It's simple to set up.
- It's completely portable. You can switch jobs as many times as you like, and not lose a penny of benefits or interrupt your accumulation plan. Additionally, there is no additional paperwork. Your investments just stay where they are, working away to provide for your eventual retirement.
- It's not associated with your employer in any way. Your employer can go right down the tubes and your IRA plan doesn't miss a beat.
- You are always 100% vested. It's always your money. In a qualified plan, it's possible to be a covered employee without receiving any benefits, and if you leave before vested, you may forfeit your entire account. This really hurts job-hoppers. (You are always 100% vested in your contributions to a pension plan, but not necessarily vested in the company contributions. So, if you are making contributions to your company 401[k] plan, relax.)
- Subject to any tax penalties, you can always reach the IRA balance for emergencies. However, do not think about robbing the kitty unless there is a really dire emergency. Having said that, it's comforting to know you can access it if you really need it.
- There are significant estate planning advantages: You can pass it on to your spouse without any income tax until withdrawn; with a little planning, you can even pass it on to future generations while preserving the tax-deferred nature. Additionally, you may find that your IRA has much less-restrictive beneficiary selections than a corporate plan, which could be important for complex estate needs or larger estates.

 Do-It-Yourself

www.Sink-Swim.com

RMD and Stretch IRA Calculator: Use this calculator to help determine how you can stretch out your retirement plan distributions for as long as possible.

On the other hand:

- Depending on your state of residence, creditor protection may not be as bulletproof as a "qualified plan." If you are a high-profile litigation target, and can't get sufficient insurance, you may want to favor a "qualified" plan whenever it's available.
- As captain of this ship, it's up to you to make wise investment decisions, or hire competent professionals to help.
- You must arrange to fund the IRA. One of the big advantages of a corporate plan can be automatic deductions and contributions. If you lack the discipline to make the contributions without a payroll deduction at source, you might be better off in a company supplied plan.
- Allowable contributions and/or deductions may be higher in other qualified plans.

IRAs have two uses: Either they are an annual, tax-favored savings account for retirement, or they are a "rollover" account for distributions of qualified plans when you separate from service or retire. You can use the same IRA for both. So, if you have any IRA open, you can roll over a pension plan into it when you change jobs or retire.

Setting Up Your IRA

You can set up your IRA at any discount brokerage house like Schwab, TD Ameritrade, or Fidelity, just to name a few. Or go directly to a good no-load family of mutual funds like Vanguard, USAA, or TIAA-Cref, which offer some of the best funds available to retail investors or investors not using a professional advisor.

Types of IRAs

There are two basic flavors of IRA: Regular and Roth. You can have both, but you must have separate accounts. You cannot co-mingle Roth and Regular, but you wouldn't want to anyway. If you are making annual contributions, you can split your deposit (choose one or the other), but you can't exceed the annual contribution limits by having two accounts.

Regular

The Regular IRA provides for a tax deduction against earned income, grows tax deferred until withdrawal, and then is fully income taxable. Early withdrawals (prior to age 59½) may be subject to penalties, but there are a number of exceptions, which are covered elsewhere in the book. When you reach age 70½, you will have to begin to take withdrawals over the rest of your lifetime. After all, Uncle Sam hasn't gotten a chance to tax these funds yet, and you can't expect him to wait forever.

You Are Not Covered by a Plan

No matter what your income, if you are not covered by a plan, and have "earned" income, you can have a Regular IRA. That's $5,000 a year, or $6,000 if you are over age 50, that you can put away on a tax-favored basis to fund your retirement. Spouses who aren't covered by a plan can have one, too (up to certain income limits, described next), even if they make no income. Over time, $10,000 to $12,000 adds up to a fair chunk of change! Table 15.1 assumes an 8% net return.

Table 15.1   Assumed Growth of Regular IRA Contributions

Years	$5,000 Per Year Contribution	$10,000 Per Year Contribution
5	$29,333	$58,666
10	$72,433	$144,866
15	$135,761	$271,521
20	$228,810	$457,620
25	$365,529	$731,059
30	$566,416	$1,132,832

The IRA enables people who change jobs and, as a result, are not covered by a retirement plan during the transition, to continue growing their retirement accounts. Otherwise, a job change might result in as much as two years lost contributions to your retirement accumulation. You can't afford that kind of interruption to your retirement investment accounts.

You Are Covered by Your Company Plan

Even if you are covered by a plan, and you decide not to participate, or you want to save more than the plan allows, the IRA is a good choice depending on your income.

Table 15.2 displays the income limits for 2008. Above the full deduction limits, there is a phase-out band where partial deductions are still possible.

Table 15.2   Income Limits for Tax Deductions for IRAs if You Are Covered by a Company Plan

Status	Full Deduction	Partial Deduction
Married Joint Return	Up to $85,000	$85,000–$103,000
Single	Up to $53,000	$53,000–$62,000
Married Filing Separate	Up to $10,000	N/A

A Spouse Is Not Covered by a Plan

If one spouse is covered by a qualified plan, but the other spouse is not, the spouse not covered (even if the spouse is not employed outside of the home) can have a deductible IRA up to the following income limits (see Table 15.3). Not nearly enough couples take advantage of this provision. It's a no-brainer, slam-dunk decision!

Table 15.3   Income Limits for Tax Deductions for IRAs if a Spouse Is Not Covered by a Plan

| Status | Income: Modified AGI | |
	Full Deduction	Partial Deduction
Married Joint Return	Up to $159,000	$159,000–$166,000
Single	N/A	N/A
Married Filing Separate	Up to $10,000	N/A

Roth IRAs

Depending on your income, you might be able to fund a Roth IRA. Congress felt that the Roth was too good of a deal to extend to higher-income taxpayers, so they placed lower caps on it, as shown in Table 15.4.

Table 15.4   Income Limits to Fund a Roth IRA

	Income: Modified AGI	
Status	**Full Contribution**	**Partial Contribution**
Married Joint Return	Up to $159,000	$159,000–$166,000
Single	$101,000	$114,000
Married Filing Separate	Up to $10,000	N/A

The difference is that instead of a tax deduction for your contribution, you get *tax-free* distributions later. It's important to understand that if your tax rate stays the same, it doesn't make a penny's difference to your retirement income picture whether you use a traditional or Roth IRA. Your net or after-tax income on withdrawals will be the same in either case.

Do-It-Yourself

www.Sink-Swim.com

Roth IRA Calculator: Use this calculator to compare the Roth IRA to an ordinary taxable investment.

Roth vs. Traditional IRA: Use this calculator to determine which IRA may be right for you.

If your tax rate goes up when you distribute the account later after retirement, you will be happy. Many believe that the current low tax rate is not sustainable—at least you wouldn't want to bet the farm that it is. Having a Roth for at least part of your retirement investments hedges against possible tax increases later.

Another great use for a Roth IRA is for young people who haven't reached their full income potential. At low income tax rates, the value of the tax deduction given up by using a Roth is negligible. Later, when they withdraw the funds tax-free that would have otherwise been taxed at a high rate, they will receive substantial tax benefits. In essence, they would have leveraged the tax code by the amount of the difference in their contribution and withdrawal tax rates. That's very powerful. For instance, if you are in a 15% tax bracket now, the value of a $1,000 tax deduction is only $150. Let's say that over time, your Roth grows to $5,000. If you forgo the tax deduction and opt for the Roth IRA, when you take it out after retirement, you keep the entire $5,000 no matter how high your current tax bracket. If you had taken advantage of the Regular IRA's tax benefit, you would have saved $150, but you would be faced with tax on the entire $5,000 when you withdraw it. So, the amount in your hands after tax would be far less.

Roth IRAs offer some benefits for your estate. In essence, you have prepaid the income tax on the entire amount for your heirs. The ability to stretch the tax-free distributions across at least two generations is very powerful. Additionally, there are no forced withdrawals at age 59½. These advantages may or may not be an important issue for you, but it's an added benefit.

Contributions to a Roth IRA can always be withdrawn tax free. But, the earnings must remain in the account until the account holder reaches age 59½, or five years after deposit—whichever is later—to receive tax-free treatment.

The ability to withdraw contributions tax-free makes them a great way to accomplish multiple goals in a tax-preferred manner. Suppose, for example, after a number of years of contributions, you withdrew those contributions to fund your daughter's college education while leaving the earnings to compound tax-free for your later retirement.

Non–Tax-Deductible IRAs

The short answer is: Don't bother.

With no tax deduction going in, and full income tax treatment coming out, you would be far better off investing in a reasonably tax-efficient index fund. A non–tax-deductible IRA turns growth of your funds—which should have been taxed at very favorable long-term capital gains rates—into ordinary income tax when the funds are distributed. On the other hand, with an equity index fund, there is little turnover inside the fund, so there is little tax-drag along the way, as long as the fund is held. When the shares are sold later to provide income, most of the realized gains are subject to capital gains tax.

As an added benefit, you don't have to put up with any of the IRA restrictions that traditional IRAs have for early withdrawals or forced withdrawals at age 70½. Additionally, your non-deductible IRA introduces reporting and tax-filing issues that are a continuing nuisance.

There is one possible reason to consider a non–tax-deductible IRA: You might want to convert it to a Roth later. However, it is most likely not worth the trouble.

In addition to tax deferral of all gains and income inside the IRA, traditional IRAs offer current tax deductions. Roth IRAs offer tax-free distributions and generous estate planning opportunities. These compelling advantages are not provided with a non-deductible IRA.

Tax deferral is a powerful wealth accumulation technique. So, at first blush, non-deductible IRA deferral is an attractive feature, but it comes with several costs that you should consider:

- **Loss of capital gains treatment:** Accumulation inside the IRA grows deferred, but all distributions are subject to ordinary income tax to the owner. This could double the tax on distributions when compared to the simple liquidation of an asset held for appreciation (that is, a stock or index mutual fund that would qualify for long-term capital gains tax treatment).

- **Premature distribution tax penalty:** Like other retirement plans, a distribution prior to age 59½ may subject the owner to a 10% penalty on top of income tax on the distribution.

- **Forced distributions at age 70½:** Your accumulations will be subject to the Minimum Required Distribution regulations along with all your other traditional IRA and pension plans. This distribution pattern may not fit your needs at the time.

- **Loss in step up in basis at death:** Your IRA will be subject to both estate tax and income tax. Your beneficiaries will pay income tax on any funds that they withdraw, diminishing the value of the account to them.

- **Accounting and reporting complications:** You may not pick and choose your tax treatment when you take a distribution. Each distribution from *any* IRA must be pro-rated between non-deductible contributions and taxable amounts for *all* accounts. At best, these tax preparation complications are annoying and frustrating. At worst, they can be costly in terms of additional accountant's fees during retirement.

On the other hand, if instead of a non-deductible IRA, you simply purchased a tax-managed index fund, you would have capital gains treatment, no premature distribution tax penalty, no forced distributions, better tax treatment for your estate, and simplified tax reporting—and you can put away as much as you like.

So, although traditional and Roth IRAs are favored, the appeal of non-deductible IRAs is dubious and severely limited. Without either current deductions or tax-free distributions, the non-deductible IRA loses its pizzazz.

Rollover IRA

IRAs have another function. If you are entitled to a lump-sum distribution when you leave an employer with a qualified plan, you can simply transfer it to an existing or new IRA. Don't worry about co-mingling rollover IRAs and the traditional IRA. That restriction went away some years ago. But, you can't co-mingle a Roth and traditional accounts.

Make sure that your rollover qualifies as a "trustee-to-trustee" transfer. Don't take personal possession of a check made out to you, or you might be in for an unpleasant tax surprise. Make sure it's made out to the receiving institution for the IRA—not you personally.

By the way, you wouldn't want to roll over your non-deductible contributions if you made any. Take them as a separate check and invest them in a regular brokerage account. However, the accumulated gains on the non-deductible contributions can and should be rolled over to your IRA.

Rollover IRAs—A Case of Outright Theft

You may need to transfer assets from one qualified account (such as a 401[k]) into another qualified account (such as an IRA). In so doing, you should always elect a "trustee-to-trustee" transfer. To do this, simply ask for the proper paperwork from the financial institution that is the custodian of the IRA into which you want to rollover money. In a trustee-to-trustee transfer, the funds go directly from one financial institution to the other. This is important. If you receive the money, the IRS will consider it to be a distribution subject to taxation and possible penalties, unless you roll it over to another IRA within 60 days. If, despite this warning, you receive the funds directly, and want to roll them over to another IRA yourself, you should only deposit the money with a bank or financial institution you know to be trustworthy, and obtain a receipt at the time of the deposit. Never pay it to a third-party and trust them to deposit for you. If you do, you open yourself up to becoming a victim of fraud. That is what happened to my former client.

The former client is a 46-year-old widow and mother of five children, whom I will call Mary. Mary received a distribution check from her deceased husband's 401(k) plan. She had become acquainted through her church with some people who presented themselves as financial advisors. Through their financial advisory company, they promised to help people like Mary get out of debt and manage their money. Unfortunately, however, they were thieves. Mary turned over her distribution check to one of these thieves, expecting him to deposit it into a newly set-up IRA account at a reputable brokerage firm. One of the thieves was a registered representative of the brokerage firm. The brokerage firm is a reputable firm with a name that most people would recognize. A rollover IRA account had been opened in Mary's name at this brokerage firm. Mary received an impressive-looking brochure that described how Mary and this brokerage firm would soon be "working together." The rollover check was made payable to the brokerage firm for the benefit of Mary. But the check never got there. It was fraudulently endorsed and deposited in an "omnibus" account in the name of the thieves' company in a far-away state. From there, Mary's funds were withdrawn and their whereabouts are unknown. Mary first learned that something was wrong when she checked her account and was shocked to discover that it had a zero balance. Instead of watching her money grow, she was filling out fraud affidavits and getting the runaround.

Fortunately for her, she was able to recover her money from the bank that cashed the check with a forged endorsement and from the brokerage firm that opened the rollover IRA account. Many of her friends, however, were not so lucky, and one of them lost her house and had to file for bankruptcy. Even more tragic is that the thief never spent a night in jail. I have learned not to count on the police when it comes to white collar crimes.

—*Contributed by Jason Doss*

Keep Up to Date

The IRS and Congress change the rules almost every year. Believe it or not, usually the changes make it more taxpayer friendly. To keep up with the latest, and learn more about how IRAs work, check out IRS Pub 590. It's very well put together, exceptionally clear, a wealth of knowledge, revised annually, and available for free on the Internet. Additionally, it has all the worksheets you need. Just google "IRS Pub 590," and it will pop right up. You will be an IRA wizard!

Summary

This lesson provided you with a high-level overview to encourage you to use IRAs whenever you get the chance. If the "average" American family put away an additional $5,000 to $10,000 a year, our retirement system and our citizens would be in much better financial shape. Remember, in the sink or swim environment, if you don't do it, no one is going to do it for you.

Lesson 16

Retirement Planning for the Self-Employed

Like many people, more than a few self-employed professionals haven't saved enough for retirement. But, unlike most corporate types, self-employed professionals with no employees can design almost any kind of pension that they want.

The advantages of pension plans are obvious: forced savings, tax deductions, tax deferral of gains, and the ability to pass on tax-deferred assets to future generations. You may think pension plans are only for employees of large corporations. Wrong! A single-participant plan is very easy, economical, and effective to set up.

In the distant past, when it came to retirement plan options, the self-employed or members of a partnership were at a distinct disadvantage relative to corporations. Although over time those restrictions have been removed, the perception of limited choices still lingers. That's unfortunate because now you have plan flexibility that would make the average corporate employee turn green with envy.

It's great being the sole decision maker. You can design a plan that meets your needs exactly without negotiating with others who have different objectives and financial situations. And with no employees, there are no pesky top-heavy or cross-testing issues that large plans have to work around and that complicate plan design and administration. Best of all, 100% of the pension deposit goes directly to your own account.

Do-It-Yourself

www.Sink-Swim.com

Individual 401(k) Contribution Comparison: Use this calculator to determine your maximum individual 401(k) contribution as compared to three other possible plan options.

Designing and maintaining your own plan doesn't have to be time consuming or expensive. All the major discount brokerages have a full spectrum of pre-approved plans that you can adopt with just a few checkmarks. Pre-approval means that the IRS has already accepted the plan, so that the hassle of filing for a "determination" letter is not required. Opening an account for most pension plans shouldn't take more than a few minutes.

Unless you have complex needs, retirement plans can be very economical. For instance, Vanguard will set up a profit-sharing plan for you with their funds that enables you to tax defer up to 25% of your net income (with a limit of $46,000 in 2008) for no additional administration or custody fees. At the end of the year, they send you all the information you need to file the required IRS form 5500. Alternatively, you can use TD Waterhouse or Fidelity Brokerage to open up the entire universe of investment choices.

The variety of plans to choose from is mind-numbing and includes IRA, Roth IRA, Simplified Employee Pension (SEP-IRA), Savings Incentive Match Plan for Employees (Simple IRA), 401(k), Roth 401(k), profit sharing, money purchase pension plan, and defined benefit plan. If you find the benefits and features of the options confusing, the Department of Labor publishes a concise table comparing plans at www.dol.gov/elaws/pwba/plans/final.asp.

The 401(k) has two neat properties that are certainly worth considering: First, when you are more than 50 years old, you can make an additional $5,000 a year "catch-up" contribution to your plan. Next, as of January 1, 2006, you can make Roth contributions to your plan. Although these get no current deductions, the funds can later be withdrawn tax-free, and they are never subject to the minimum distribution rules at age 70½. If you expect to be in a higher income bracket later, or if you predict tax rates in general will go up, this is an especially good way to leverage the tax code.

---

www.Sink-Swim.com

Do-It-Yourself

Roth 401(k) or Traditional 401(k): Use this calculator to help determine if a traditional 401(k) or Roth 401(k) might be best for you.

With all those choices available, how do you decide which one to select? A good starting point is to determine how much you can save comfortably for your retirement goal, and then pick the least cumbersome plan that allows for that level of savings. As in many other facets of life, simplicity is best.

If you are older, behind in your retirement savings, and would like to sock away lots of your income, consider defined benefit plans. Although large corporations are terminating their plans en masse, small employers are taking advantage of the ability to shelter significant amounts of income for their highly compensated principals. For instance, a recently designed single-participant plan for a self-employed 55-year-old physician/consultant allowed the deferring of income of slightly more than $162,000 a year for the next ten years.

Don't get bogged down in minutia. The overwhelming issue is not the fine points of difference between pension plans, but whether or not you are saving enough so that you can live with a certain amount of class and comfort later in life.

Unless you are very confident of your investment skills, it makes sense to utilize an investment advisor to tend your nest egg. Just make sure you avoid commission-based brokers and stick with professional fee-only advisors so that you get objective advice. For a match to qualified professional fee-only advisors, check www.napfa.org or www.paladinregistry.com. The additional cost of objective professional advice is well worth it.

Lesson 17───────────

How Does Your Plan Stack Up?

Retirement plans are all about creation, and protection of wealth with the end goal to provide a secure and bountiful lifetime income after retirement. Yes, the tax benefits are nice, but that's not the objective. If the plan is poorly constructed, the tax benefits can be swamped by additional costs and poor performance. Almost all plans provide access to fancy websites with numerous bells and whistles. Those bright, shiny objects must not distract you from the primary purpose of the plan, which is to provide economical, effective investments.

Employee-funded retirement plans run the gamut from great to awful. Unfortunately, the quality of the plan is most often not within the control of the individual employee. They receive whatever crumbs the employer feels like, on a take-it-or-leave-it basis. Unfortunately, additionally, there are no recognized standards for the employee and management to use as a yardstick. Although ERISA requires fiduciary behavior by plan sponsors, those standards are little understood by management, and most often ignored.

At its best, where the plan sponsor has been a prudent fiduciary for the plan participants, the employee-funded plan can be made to do a decent job. It offers automatic savings, tax advantages, and creditor protection. In particular, this plan can be an excellent accumulation vehicle for younger employees, who have long time horizons before their retirements.

How can you judge if it is worth it to contribute to your plan? You need to evaluate it just like any other investment plan. It should be effective, low cost, and low risk. If not, don't contribute. The following sections discuss things you should look for.

Total Expenses

Expenses include fund fees, administration costs, commissions, investment advisor fees, mortality and expense charges, custody fees, and account charges. If the total costs of all the various parts exceed 1.5% of the assets under management of the plan per year, the employee might rightfully wonder if assets are being squandered.

Some plan sponsors subsidize investment advisor fees and administrative costs that could reduce the costs that the employee pays by as much as 1% per year. However, many bad plans have total costs that exceed 3%, all borne by the employee. No one should want to participate in an account with that level of expense. Fees and expenses of that magnitude suck any profit potential right out of the plan.

---

www.Sink-Swim.com

Do-It-Yourself

Compare Investment Fees: Even a small difference in the fees you pay on your investments can add up over time. Use this calculator to see how different fees impact your investment strategy!

Compare Savings Rates: Even a small difference in the interest you are paid on your savings can add up over time. Use this calculator to see how different savings rates can impact your savings strategy!

Quality Fund Choices

Ideally each fund represents an asset class, and is low cost, low turnover, and widely diversified. Index funds are the preferred solution for each asset class. Mutual funds, separate accounts, co-mingled trusts, and other pooled assets are an important component of total costs. There should be no commissions, 12(b)-1 fees, or back-end surrender charges. Together these charges alone can add up to costs exceeding 3% per year. For example, plans on which the author's firm advises have total annual, weighted, average mutual fund costs of less than one-half percent per year, yet provide global stock exposure, real estate, and commodities futures exposure.

Adequate Funds Choices to Diversify the Portfolio Properly

Participants should be able to diversify their equity portfolios globally within the plan, and control the risk-reward character of the portfolio with a high-quality, short-term bond fund. A really good plan might additionally include a real estate fund, small and value funds in both foreign and domestic markets, and a commodities futures fund as options.

Suggested Asset Allocations

The days when a plan could throw 200 mutual funds at participants without guidance are long gone. The average American employee is not a qualified investment advisor. Few of us are born knowing the intricacies of portfolio construction and management.

Even professional-level employees need clear, unambiguous guidance to construct appropriate investment portfolios that will meet their changing needs as they progress through their careers. Employees need investment solutions, not overwhelming complexity.

Balanced accounts, lifecycle strategy funds, and target date funds may look like a quick fix, but they are a poor substitute for a complete, optimized, asset allocation plan. For example, the 401(k) plans that the author's firm advises provide at least five different, suggested, global asset allocation plans with differing proportions of stock and bond holdings that employees can select with a single checkmark. These are the same portfolios used with our multi-millionaire clients.

Company Stock: Just Say "No"

The correct amount of company stock in a 401(k) account is zero. If company stock is offered as an option, employees should decline it. If company stock is contributed as the company match program, employees should sell it immediately; if they can't dispose of it promptly, they should consider it as close to zero in value. Employees at companies such as US Air, Enron, and Countrywide Mortgage have all had their retirement plans destroyed by the death spiral of the employer stock inside their plan. None of them expected their companies to fail and leave them destitute in the process. Don't be next year's poster child for imprudent investment.

Bells and Whistles

Almost all plans today come coupled with various kinds of technological extras. Extras are nice to have but are not nearly as important as the range of asset classes, the quality of investments offered, and the cost borne by the participant. Don't let such extras distract you from the purpose of the plan. Online access is of no value if the investment plan is defective.

Individual Advice

Under the Pension Protection Act of 2006, qualifying investment advisors may offer participants individual advice. This can be extremely helpful if the plan is otherwise worthy. However, if the advice consists of guiding you to the least-poor choices in a dismal set of plan options while generating yet another cost for your account, it may not be a benefit after all.

Company Match

Some companies provide no matching contributions at all, while other plans are so generous that they are just about irresistible.

A strong company match is a powerful incentive to participate in a well-designed pension plan. Otherwise, you would be leaving money on the table (and generally, it's a bad idea to leave money on the table). But unless the plan is superior as an investment plan standing on its own, don't contribute more than necessary to get the match.

Lesson 18 ——————————————

What Can Go Wrong

DB Plan Termination

Your grandfather's defined benefit (DB) pension plan may be an endangered species. DB pension plans subject companies to high costs and risk that many prefer not to assume. As a result, it's becoming increasingly common to see such plans eliminated.

Voluntary Freezes or Terminations

If companies freeze existing plans, the plans continue, but employee participants accrue no further benefits. The company may need to make further contributions if the plan is under-funded when frozen.

If the company terminates the plan, the accrued benefits (including all unvested benefits) must either be paid out as a lump-sum equivalent, or the plan must purchase a commercial annuity from an insurance company. It goes without saying that the plan must be fully funded when terminated.

Usually, but not in all cases, the company then starts some form of defined contribution (DC) plan to take its place. It's unlikely that the benefits of the two plans will be entirely equal. DB plans favor older, long-term employees. Such employees may be considerably worse off, while younger employees may find that, potentially, they may have higher benefits projections. In a famous recent case, older IBM employees successfully argued that the conversion to a "cash balance" pension was blatantly discriminatory. However, the decision is unlikely to stop the trend away from DB pensions.

Distress or Involuntary Terminations

Occasionally, companies fail outright, taking their DB plans down with them. ERISA established the Pension Board Guarantee Corporation (PBGC) to provide employees with at least partial insurance of their accrued benefits in DB plans. Today, almost a million present and future retirees look to the PBGC for their retirement benefits.

Single employer plans pay an annual per participant fee of $19.00, as well as 0.9% of any amount by which the plan is found to lack because it is under-funded. The premium is mandated by federal law, and has not been sufficient to cover existing liabilities. Even though the PBGC itself is insolvent, Congress has been reluctant to raise the premiums, perhaps fearing that it might accelerate the trend away from DB plans.

When plans do not have sufficient assets to pay all its intended benefits and the employers are in such distress that continuing their plans might cause the companies to fail, the company can petition the PBGC for a distress termination. In a distress termination, the PBGC steps in to pay "guaranteed" benefits and attempts to recover the balance from the employer, either over time or in bankruptcy.

Should the PBGC find that it is in the best interest of the employees, the plan, or the PBGC itself, it can take over a plan without the employer's consent. Finally, if a firm suspends operation or cannot continue as a going business, the PBGC will step in to take over the plan.

The stock market decline of 2000–2002 devastated many DB pension plans. Much of this grief was self-induced. The plan fiduciaries, their actuaries, and the Labor Department, all lulled by long market advances, increased rate of return assumptions to reduce estimated annual costs. Then they took higher levels of risk to attempt to meet their rate of return assumptions. Finally, they were the victims of inappropriate asset allocation that failed to diversify their portfolios properly. When the market tanked, some found themselves suddenly underwater at just the time that their businesses were in distress. In some well-publicized cases, the pension liabilities exceeded the net worth of the companies.

You shouldn't be shocked to discover that many companies view bankruptcy as a great way to unload their pension liabilities on the taxpayer, clean up their balance sheet, lower costs, and compete against other companies that are trying to do the right thing by maintaining their plans and keeping their promises to their employees.

The airlines and steel companies, already financially weak, were particularly hard hit after 9/11. Recent legislation relaxed funding standards for these two industries. They will be allowed temporary additional under-funding in the hopes that they will recover. This is a massive bet for the government. If the firms do not recover, PBGC will be forced to take on plans that are even more severely under-funded than they are today. With the PBGC itself already severely in the red, the prospect of allowing any employers to under-fund their plans further may come back to bite the agency with a vengeance.

Highly compensated employees will find that the PBGC guarantee covers only a small portion of their benefits. They can be financially devastated by a plan termination. Although plans can fund to a maximum of $185,000 per year at normal retirement, the PBGC maximum guaranteed benefit in 2008 is $51,750 per year for those who retire at age 65.

When plans offered by distressed companies offer a lump-sum benefit, the threat of possible plan termination can cause a "run on the bank," as senior employees attempt to secure their lump sum prior to the termination. For instance, Delta Airlines had 300 pilots retire in June 2004 alone, with 266 of them early. Unfortunately, every employee that succeeds in securing a lump-sum payment further weakens the fund for remaining participants.

Interestingly, if companies maintain multiple plans for different employee groups, they may have the option of picking and choosing which pension to terminate. For instance, US Air, operating under Chapter 11 bankruptcy, was allowed a distress termination of the Pilot's Pension while continuing other employees' pensions. (Senior pilots found their benefits cut by more than $100,000 per year! Roughly, that's about a $2,000,000 decrease in assets that had accrued over a 30+ year career for each of those professional pilots!)

The PBGC process is often arbitrary and capricious. When challenged, its representatives have proven to be tireless litigators. For instance: When the PBGC took over the Pilot's Pension at Eastern Airlines, it was almost fully funded, while other groups were greatly under-funded. The pilots had, through the collective bargaining process, negotiated for increased funding for their plan that was paid for by reducing their pay. Nevertheless, PBGC promptly stole the pilot's funds to distribute to less fully funded Eastern employees' plans. The theft impoverished the pilot group, but reduced the PBGC's liability for the other plans. This theft was never challenged in court.

When Pan American Airlines folded, its Pilot's Pension plan was under-funded. However, during the administrative process, the stock market rebounded, greatly enhancing funding levels. The PBGC kept the additional funds and argued successfully in court that they were not fiduciaries of the plan, but its insurer. Pilots received minimum benefits rather than the benefits the plan could have provided with the enhanced asset values.

Conclusions

The trend away from the traditional DB plan is probably irreversible as companies attempt to reduce costs and avoid possible future liabilities for under-funding. Employees currently covered under DB plans must consider in their planning that their anticipated benefits may possibly be reduced in the future. This is of particular concern in distressed industries where highly compensated employees could experience draconian cuts. In any event, as in almost all other aspects of DB pension plans, employees are along for the ride with little or no control over their plans.

Defined Contribution: Plan Sponsor Failure

If you are a participant in a DB plan, and your employer fails or terminates the plan, it can ruin your whole day. (See "DB Plan Termination," earlier in the lesson.) However, absent outright fraud or theft, the failure of a DC sponsor is not usually nearly so traumatic.

Assuming that the required contributions were made on schedule, a defined contribution plan can never be under-funded. Unlike a DB plan, the employer is not promising any particular benefit. Although the employer must petition the Department of Labor for a plan termination, the procedure is relatively simple compared to a DB plan. No actuarial calculations are required, and government processing is usually not delayed unreasonably. Whatever funds are in your account will become immediately vested upon plan termination and eventually paid out to you.

If your plan is invested in liquid securities such as mutual funds or separately managed accounts, payout should be fairly straightforward. The accounts are valued as of a termination date and distributions made to the participants. That's the normal course of events. But there are a limited number of unfortunate exceptions.

In a few cases, companies may not have made required contributions to their plans, or have stolen from them. Although this is unusual, it's not impossible. The following warning signs are from a Department of Labor article, "Warning Signs That 401(k) Contributions Are Being Misused"[1]:

- Your 401(k) or individual account statement is consistently late or comes at irregular intervals.
- Your account balance does not appear to be accurate.
- Your employer failed to transmit your contribution to the plan on a timely basis.
- A significant drop in account balance that cannot be explained by normal market ups and downs.
- 401(k) or individual account statement shows your contribution from your paycheck was not made.
- Investments listed on your statement are not what you authorized.
- Former employees are having trouble getting their benefits paid on time or in the correct amounts.
- Unusual transactions, such as a loan to the employer, a corporate officer, or one of the plan trustees.
- Frequent and unexplained changes in investment managers or consultants.
- Your employer has recently experienced severe financial difficulty.

Unfortunately, if there are illiquid investments such as real estate or limited partnerships, payout may be delayed until the properties can be unwound. This was the case with the Eastern Pilots Pension Plan, where the Air Line Pilots Association had "cleverly" invested more than 90% of the fund in raw undeveloped land. In that sorry case, it took more than 10 years for the participants to be paid out and

---

[1] U.S. Department of Labor, "Warning Signs That 401(k) Contributions Are Being Misused," http://www.dol.gov/ebsa/publications/10warningsigns.html

the plan terminated. Even worse, the land had been systematically overvalued by the trustees. The pilots never recovered the full amount that they had been led to expect. Fortunately, these gross lapses in fiduciary responsibility are rare.

The Enron example provided a stark lesson in the importance of avoiding company stock in your retirement plan. Losing your job and having your 401(k) crater at the same time is the financial equivalent of the perfect storm. It's a disaster from which you may never recover. To the extent that Enron employees chose that investment over a diversified account within the plan, it was self-induced injury. Management strongly advised employees to fund their plans solely with Enron stock, a gross abuse of their fiduciary duties that was entirely self-serving. Wherever possible, reduce your holdings of employer stock in your personal accounts and retirement plans to zero.

Because many company plans hold accounts for past employees, over time some of these accounts become "orphans" when the plan sponsor loses track of those employees' current contact information. If a plan terminates and those orphans cannot be found, they are likely to have their accounts liquidated and rolled into an IRA with a third party. The default investment will most likely be cash, which is hardly ever optimal because it is guaranteed never to experience real growth. Strange as it may sound, there are many orphan accounts nationwide. The lesson here is to keep your former employers notified as to your current address. If the plan gives you the option, a rollover into an account you control might be your best course.

In a very few rare cases, the liquidation of a company leaves the pension plan an orphan with nobody to wind up its affairs or make distributions. In that event, the Department of Labor will appoint a third-party, independent trustee to terminate the plan.

In most cases when a plan terminates, your best option is to roll over the account immediately to an IRA and invest it for your future needs. A rollover often enables you to reduce costs, exactly tailor the account to your situation, and upgrade investment choices.

Lesson 19 ——————————————————

Should You Contribute to It?

The knee-jerk advice from the media and financial planner community is to contribute the maximum you can afford to your 401(k) plan. After all, at their best, retirement plans offer some significant advantages. However, not all plans capture all the potential benefits, and some squander them entirely with high costs and poor investment choices.

None of the private pension plans, whether defined benefit or defined contribution plans, will work unless the plan sponsors/fiduciaries do their job. There is precious little evidence that this is happening. Although there are some exceptions, we also see massive failure of fiduciary standards. A huge number of private pensions are disgracefully bad, incapable of delivering retirement security or decent returns for participants. Waste, corruption, mismanagement, and failure to adhere to elementary fiduciary standards cost American retirees hundreds of billions of dollars!

But, wait. The biggest advantage to any retirement plan is forced savings. Either you put money away, or your employer puts it away for you. In either case, if nobody puts anything away, there is nothing at retirement.

Another often-cited advantage is deferral of taxation on realized investment gains inside the plan. This advantage is not trivial but is directly related to the turnover within the plan, as well as the interest and dividends that the plan earns. An efficient portfolio outside of a pension plan will minimize this drag but cannot entirely eliminate it.

Current deductions against earned income are more psychological than real unless your retirement income tax bracket is lower than your working bracket. Given the substantial deficit and funding problems built into our current fiscal policy, the chances of future tax increases are all too real. If your retirement tax bracket turns out to be higher, then you will have inadvertently done yourself in. The math is pretty simple. A deduction now at any rate, followed by a tax on distribution at the same rate, is a zero tax benefit no matter how much the account has grown in the meantime. True, you have deferred the tax on your income now, but paid it back plus tax on the earnings later. You are no better off or worse off than without the deferral.

Unless your plan qualifies as "great," then you may not want to consider contributing any more than the minimum to get the match. If there is no match, you may be better off saving in a tax-efficient brokerage account. This presumes that you have the discipline to contribute to an outside account, and not raid the cookie jar to purchase toys.

Lesson 20————————————

Alternatives to Qualified Plans

The 401(k), 403(b), and 457 plans are employee-funded savings plans. They are investment plans first and foremost. If they can't pass muster as a comprehensive investment plan, no amount of tax deferral is going to turn that frog into a prince. Merely having a plan is not the same as having a good plan. As investment solutions, plans divide themselves into the good, the bad, and the ugly. Because you have to provide most of the money from your own pocket, you must decide if the plan is worth participating in. Remember, tax advantages are not the whole picture. The chief tax advantage of a qualified retirement plan is deferral of tax on investment earnings. And by far the biggest advantage of a "qualified" employment savings plan is that it makes savings automatic. That's a good thing, but you can perhaps get a better result if you set up another more effective investment plan.

Many employee savings plans can't stand on their own as superior investment programs. The knee-jerk advice to max out your plan might not be the best possible course.

The Good

Of course, some plans are world-class, with low costs, superior funds, and great underlying features. If the employer subsidizes the plan further by paying all or part of the administration and investment advice costs, so much the better. Of course, if it's a great plan, you can't go wrong by maxing out your contributions. Lucky you! Go for it!

The Bad

Some plans are tolerable with a few good choices. Perhaps they have strong employer matches, which overcome some of their flaws. Individuals are often in the position of having to select the least awful choice from a dismal lineup. But, forget about being able to construct an appropriate asset allocation plan within the plan. Sometimes you must invest the minimum to get the employer match and invest the rest of your retirement savings elsewhere.

The Ugly

And finally, some plans are simply not worth investing in. The plan is expensive, the choices are awful, and the match by the employer is little to none. The author routinely sees 401(k) plans where the total cost approaches and even exceeds 3% of the entire employee's account each year! How do you think anybody can meet their reasonable retirement objectives with 3% of the account being sucked out each year? In some cases, the annual account expenses can far exceed the employer's match.

Alternatives

If your employee-funded pension plan stinks, you have alternatives.

The first and best option should be to work with your employer. Depending on the circumstances, you might either urge the company to offer a plan, or improve an existing plan. Squeaky wheels get oiled far more often than silent ones. So, squeak up.

Most employers have a strong preference for happy, secure employees. So they might be sensitive to your needs for a decent retirement plan. But, it's unlikely that they will spontaneously decide to offer a plan or improve an existing plan without a little prodding. After all, they are in the business of making widgets. Although the quality of the 401(k) plan might not exactly be topmost of their concerns, they really don't want employees to be unhappy with the benefit package—and in most cases, they are participants, too.

Even in large companies, many professional HR people may not understand the fiduciary obligations of a plan sponsor. Frequently they are unaware of the basics of plan design and funding. To put it bluntly, they may be completely clueless about plan defects. However, if you show them ways to improve the plan while cutting costs and reducing the employer's liability, they just might get motivated.

Employers really should be aware that if they squander employee pension funds, they are personally liable under ERISA and a few hundred years of common law. Perhaps the securities litigators are the best hope to clean up the swamp. Certainly, poorly run pensions are a juicy target for class action lawsuits.

A Game Plan if Your Employee-Funded Plan Falls Short

You have to play the hand that you are dealt. If your company pension plans falls short, you can't just throw up your hands and quit. That's no way to retire in style! You have very good alternatives. Take control of your future and act on your alternatives:

- If the plan is mediocre, perhaps with a strong match, find the best choices (or the least awful), invest the minimum to get the match, and look for other outside investment opportunities.
- If your spouse has a better plan, cram everything you can into it. Together, you might be able to meet the family retirement savings goal.

- If your income is within the IRS limits, set up an IRA for yourself. Don't forget that if your spouse isn't covered, you might be able to set up an IRA for your spouse, too. Consider the Roth IRA if your income falls within appropriate limits.

- Invest in a tax-efficient family of index funds. You want the minimum tax drag from your portfolio, and the minimum cost. Just two index funds, like the Vanguard Total Stock Market and Total International Stock Index, provide effective, economical, tax-efficient, global equity diversification.

- Whatever you do, don't invest in an individual fixed or variable annuity for your retirement investment account. That's a product that exists only to make insurance agents and stockbrokers rich.

Summary

A bad employee-funded retirement plan won't get you where you want to go. And you shouldn't invest in it if it doesn't stack up on its own merits as a superior investment plan. Take the time to evaluate your plan and decide if you want to participate or not. If your employer won't fix it, you still have alternatives that make good economic sense.

Lesson 21————————————————

Help from the Courts

If you are at retirement and your plan has substantially underperformed or endured greater than necessary costs, you have a right to be made whole through the litigation. A couple percent of additional costs and a few years of underperformance against the appropriate benchmarks may result in your pension benefit being less than half of what it should have been.

A recent Supreme Court case (LARUE v. DEWOLFF, BOBERG & ASSOCIATES, INC., ET AL.) established the right of an individual to sue plan sponsors of 401(k) plans for any breach of their fiduciary obligations. Citing ERISA Section 409:

"Any person who is a fiduciary with respect to a plan who breaches any of the responsibilities, obligations, or duties imposed upon fiduciaries by this title shall be personally liable to make good to such plan any losses to the plan resulting from each such breach, and to restore to such plan any profits of such fiduciary which have been made through use of assets of the plan by the fiduciary, and shall be subject to such other equitable or remedial relief as the court may deem appropriate, including removal of such fiduciary. A fiduciary may also be removed for a violation of section 411 of this Act." 88 Stat. 886, 29 U. S. C. §1109(a).

This language is crystal clear. Plan sponsors of substandard plans must be hearing footsteps today. The threat of litigation and personal liability may be the only way to get the attention of some plan sponsors.

The Supreme Court ruling is a substantial motivational tool for plan sponsors, and you can hope that it will lead to overall plan improvements going forward.

Meanwhile, if you suspect your plan is seriously underperforming or subject to excessive fees, you might want to remind your employer of their legal obligations as your fiduciary. As a last resort, if you have been shortchanged, consult with appropriate legal counsel.

Please check www.Sink-Swim.com for calculators, updates, and additional information, such as articles and links to valuable outside resources. Also, read the Sink or Swim blog and join in the discussion group.

Part III

WHERE ARE YOU IN YOUR CAREER?

Certain overriding principles apply throughout your career and retirement:

- At every stage, you need to control your credit card and other consumer debts.
- Keep your estate planning up to date and make certain your beneficiary selection for your qualified plans is appropriate for your family needs.
- Make sure you are insured against accidents, disability, illness, and premature death as appropriate for your family situation.
- Take only appropriate levels of risk for your life stage.
- Manage investment risk diligently. You will never have time to make up for a catastrophic loss in your retirement portfolio.

At different stages of your career, or if you are changing jobs, there are particular things you should focus on to keep yourself on track toward your secure, comfortable, and prosperous retirement.

Lesson 22 ————————————

Early and Mid-Career

Early in your career, you are in the accumulation stage:

- It's not possible to overemphasize the importance of an early start. The magic of compounding rewards is compelling for those who keep time on their side.

 Do-It-Yourself

www.Sink-Swim.com

Don't Delay Your Savings! Waiting to begin your savings plan can have a huge impact on your results. This calculator helps show you how much postponing your savings plan can really cost.

- Save liberally.
- Lean more toward equities to accumulate enough to meet your goals.
- The longer your time horizon until retirement, the more aggressive you can afford to be with your money. If you aren't spending the money in the next few years, you shouldn't be too concerned about short-term market fluctuations.

 Do-It-Yourself

www.Sink-Swim.com

Asset Allocator: Your age, ability to tolerate risk, and several other factors are used to calculate a desirable mix of stocks, bonds, and cash.

- You still have to manage risk. Resist "taking a flier" with the idea that you have time to make up for a bad investment. You can't make up for an early portfolio implosion.

Later in the next lesson, you learn specific investment techniques that you can adopt to maximize your probability of a prosperous retirement.

You can't afford to delay your accumulation plan. Time is your biggest ally. Just do it.

Lesson 23

Changing Jobs: Smart Moves for Your Pension Plan

There are no more lifetime jobs. Career changes are the new reality. If you are changing jobs, one of the many big decisions you will face is what to do with your pension plan. You have four basic choices, each with its own pros and cons:

- Take the money.
- Leave it in your old company's pension plan.
- Roll it over into your new company's pension plan.
- Roll it over into an IRA.

---

www.Sink-Swim.com

Do-It-Yourself

401(k) Spend It or Save It Calculator: There are several ways to manage your 401(k) when you leave an employer. Making the wrong decision can cost you thousands of dollars, both in taxes and lost earnings.

How should you evaluate the options?

In each case, there are a few additional factors you need to consider, as follows:

- Outstanding loans
- Company stock

- Separation from service after age 55
- Creditor protection

You will probably find that an IRA rollover is the best choice. But, consider your options first.

Take the Money and Run!

Taking the money and spending it is not one of the smarter choices. The most important reason for not blowing the money is that you shouldn't be looting your retirement account systematically. Keeping the money growing in a tax-deferred environment until you need it for retirement is an enormous benefit. The IRS gives you this huge advantage in the hopes that the government won't have to support you on welfare tomorrow.

Just in case you didn't get the hint, the IRS has devised some pretty draconian treatments for those withdrawing funds before normal retirement age. They really don't want you to finance your next car or vacation with your pension distribution.

For starters, if you are under age 59½, the pension will be required to withhold 20% to cover part of the enormous tax you are going to owe. But, it gets worse. Because you are paying tax on the distribution at ordinary income tax rates, you might have a tax rate of up to 39% on the entire distribution. So, at the end of the year, you might very well have a severe tax deficit and penalty if you didn't properly withhold on your quarterly filings. Unless you fall under one of the exemptions for death, disability, and so on, you might also be penalized an additional 10% for early withdrawal. And, of course, if you live in a state with income tax, the state may further deplete your remaining balance.

Let's look at an example to see just how bad this might be. Sally, a 30-year-old attorney, has a pension balance of $50,000 and just got an offer from a competing firm. She thinks it might be neat to show up driving a new red Miata. Table 23.1 reflects how that would work out.

Table 23.1   Taxes and Penalties on a Premature Pension Distribution

Total Distribution	$50,000
Less 20% withholding	$10,000
Net check to Sally	$40,000
Additional taxes due (assuming 28% rate)	$4,000
Penalty tax 10%	$5,000
Net proceeds	$31,000

Almost 40% of Sally's distribution evaporated. It's gone off to the IRS, never to be seen again. In case you haven't noticed, the IRS is a one-way street. Your money can go in, but it's not coming back out!

Instead of buying the car, if Sally decides to roll over the account within the 60-day window, but after she receives the check from the plan administrator, she will have to dip into her pocket or borrow the $10,000 that was withheld in order to complete the rollover. She can file for the refund the following year when she does her taxes.

If she doesn't fund the missing $10,000, but rolls over the $40,000 net she received, she will owe taxes and possibly penalties on the $10,000 that was withheld. A trustee-to-trustee transfer avoids this problem entirely because it is a non-taxable event (or transfer).

Systematically Looting Your Retirement Funds

The real problem with these transactions is that Sally has impoverished herself in her old age. Employees who withdraw their pension funds are systematically destroying their own retirement benefits. Had she left the proceeds at work earning even 9% in a tax-deferred account, by the time she turned 60, the balance would have been $663,384. At 65, the balance should be $1,020,698, and she could comfortably withdraw $50,000 a year forever, presuming a sustainable withdrawal rate of 5% per year. Pretty expensive little red car!

Age 55 Separation from Service

If the facts are changed a little to make Sally 55 or older when she "separates from service," then because the funds come from a qualified plan, Sally receives an exemption from the 10% penalty tax. However, if the funds go into an IRA and are withdrawn prior to age 59½, the penalty would apply.

If Sally is taking an early retirement after age 55 but before age 59½, and if her plan allows it, then funding her retirement needs directly from plan distributions may in fact make sense.

Company Stock

If part of Sally's account is made up of company stock, Sally might benefit from another little-known provision called Net Unrealized Appreciation (NUA). She could withdraw just the stock and pay taxes only on the cost basis that the plan had in the stock. (The cost basis is the value of the shares when the company contributes them to the plan.) Later, when she sells the stock for whatever reason, she will pay capital gains on the difference between the cost basis and sales price. This might be very attractive to a participant with a large balance of company stock at a very low basis.

So, to use an absurd example, suppose the entire account is company stock and the basis is $1.00. Sally pays ordinary tax on $1.00 when she has the stock distributed to her. Later, when she sells it, she pays capital gains rates on the difference between the $1.00 and the sales price. In some situations where the basis is very low, this might compare favorably with a rollover on an after-tax basis. However, the benefits and costs have to be computed for each unique situation. In one case where the author testified as an expert witness, utilizing the favorable NUA tax strategy on a large distribution would have saved the employee $240,000 in income tax.

Do-It-Yourself

www.Sink-Swim.com

Company Stock Distribution Analysis Calculator: If you own company stock in a retirement plan, you might be able to take advantage of using the long-term capital gains tax rate rather than your ordinary income tax rate on this investment.

Reinvesting the Net Proceeds

Instead of the little red Miata, Sally might be considering re-investing the net proceeds to grow for retirement. However, it's unlikely that she will ever be able to make up for the loss of capital she incurs by paying the taxes so many years in advance. Deferral is a powerful wealth accumulation technique. Keeping all those dollars at work in a tax-deferred environment is a huge advantage not easily matched.

Creditor Proofing

Funds withdrawn from a qualified pension account lose their federal protection against creditors. This could be devastating if a future lawsuit award exceeds available insurance coverage, or in the event of a bankruptcy.

Conclusion

Keep time and the valuable benefit of continued deferral on your side by keeping your retirement plans at work for you. Resist the temptation to blow the money. Taking the money is not an option you should consider.

Leaving the Money in Your Old Plan

Ideally, you won't be tempted to take the money and blow it. The advantages of deferral are just too great to pass up. Having eliminated that as a possibility, let's look at whether you might consider leaving your funds with your old employer's plan.

In the vast majority of cases, employees are best served to roll over their funds. A few job changers will find that leaving their funds in their old employers' plans might meet their needs. However, each has to consider their individual circumstances to come to the right decision. Let's look at the pros and cons.

Reasons to Remain in the Old Plan

Low Costs and Wide Menu of Investment Choices

Although it's generally not the case, a few employers provide superb, low-cost plans and subsidize the administrative costs rather than pass those costs on to employees. Better 401(k) or pension plans may offer almost unlimited choices of low-cost funds from which a very sophisticated plan can be crafted. If you are satisfied with the plan costs, features, and investment choices, there may be no compelling case to withdraw your funds.

Asset Protection

Qualified pension plan assets enjoy federal protection from most creditors under ERISA. This same level of protection may not be available under your state laws for IRAs. Statutes differ from state to state. If there is a significant chance that you might have a claim that exceeds your insurance protection, and your state offers a low level of creditor protection for IRAs, you might be wise to leave your assets inside a qualified plan.

Early Retirement Between Ages 55 and 59½

Qualified plans have a big advantage over IRAs for employees who need income from their plans if they have reached age 55 when they separate from service. There is no 10% early withdrawal penalty for distributions from a qualified plan. But, once the money is rolled into an IRA, withdrawals before age 59½ are subject to the penalty unless employees qualify for one of the exemptions (death, disability, and so on) or set up a withdrawal plan under section 72(t). Because the 72(t) withdrawal plans lack flexibility, this might be an important consideration. (Note: You cannot use this feature unless you worked until age 55 and then separated from service. For instance, you couldn't separate from service at age 53, wait two years, and then begin taking penalty-free withdrawals.)

Reasons to Look Elsewhere

Your Old Employer May Force You Out

Employers aren't usually anxious to provide services to former plan participants. The time and money are direct costs of doing business, better spent on existing employees. For instance, keeping track of former employees' addresses, and providing statements, summary plan descriptions, and other required overhead mount up to a substantial sum over time. So, a majority of employers require that terminated employees make other arrangements for their accounts.

Limited Investment Choices

Few 401(k) plans provide the wealth of investment choices necessary to execute a sophisticated asset allocation plan or coordinate with other investments not held in the plan.

High Costs

Many 401(k) plan costs are unacceptably high. Total costs may easily exceed 3% per year or more. Saving one or two percent a year in plan costs can add up to a fortune over your career.

Control

401(k) plans offer little control over when and how to use the capital. On balance, this is a very good thing. Employees who use their retirement plans to finance vacations or purchase consumer goods systematically plunder their future security. On the other hand, in a dire emergency, access to the funds might be valuable. Other plans may make it difficult to re-align investment strategy to meet the participant's changing needs.

Consolidation

Today's mobile workforce job hops at a dizzying pace. Some job-hoppers find themselves with multiple retirement accounts with past employers. It quickly becomes difficult to manage all these accounts properly, design a comprehensive investment plan, or obtain a global view of account performance.

One Final Consideration: Loans

If you have an outstanding loan when you leave your old employer, you must either pay it back, or be taxed on the amount of the loan as a distribution. Loans from pension plans must be repaid by payroll deduction. If you aren't on the payroll, you can't continue the loan payments, which will trigger a distribution report to the IRS.

Rolling Your Plan into Your New Employer's Plan

The number of people who roll over their pension plans from one employer to another is very, very small. Most find that a rollover to an IRA better fits their needs. Still, in certain situations, it might be your best option.

Costs and Features

If the new plan has lower costs than an IRA might, and has all the features and investment choices you could want, then it might be worth considering.

Creditor Proofing

A direct "trustee-to-trustee" rollover between qualified plans may not be subject to your creditors. So, you continue to enjoy the same high levels of creditor proofing that a qualified plan provides in the new employer plan. This might be important if you have a potential claim that exceeds your insurance limits or an outstanding judgment, and your state protection from creditors for IRAs is weak. For most investors, it won't be a critical consideration.

Loans

If you have a loan against your old employer's plan, you must either pay it off or suffer the tax and penalties when you default. However, there may be a way to avoid this unfortunate result. Obtain a short-term loan from your bank or family, pay off the loan to the old plan, roll over the entire amount, and then take out a new loan against the new plan. This, of course, assumes that the new plan provides for loans.

Retirement Between 55 and 59½

If you plan on an early retirement between 55 and 59½, but haven't reached that age yet, you may have more favorable options under the new company's plan than under an IRA. A rollover to the new employer's plan will preserve such options.

Note: If your old employer plan contains low basis company stock, it would lose its special treatment if rolled over into either an IRA or your new company's plan. If you find that it is an advantage to take a distribution of the company stock for tax purposes, do it first, and then roll over the balance.

The Conduit IRA

If your intent is to roll over your pension plan into a future employer's plan, but don't have employment lined up yet, you can still position yourself for a later rollover. Just open an IRA or use an existing one, and then at a later time, you can roll over into the new company's plan. As you no longer have to be concerned with co-mingling funds, you don't have to set up a separate IRA just for the rollover.

The IRA Rollover

After you have considered all the other possibilities, you will most likely find that your best choice for your pension funds is the IRA rollover. Unless you fall into one of the rare situations outlined in the previous sections, the advantages are overwhelming:

- **Total Control of Investment Philosophy and Execution.** It's a rare investor who can completely construct his optimum portfolio within the confines of a pension plan. An IRA rollover with a discount brokerage house like TD Waterhouse or Fidelity offers thousands of no-load mutual funds, ETFs, individual stocks and bonds, or other investment options.

- **Costs.** By divorcing yourself from the plan's administrative costs, and selecting lower-cost funds, you can often save in excess of 2% per year. Such savings will add up to enormous benefits over your lifetime.

- **Consolidation.** One IRA rollover is a lot easier and more convenient to manage than several little pension plan accounts spread over a number of different custodians, each with different fund choices, forms, statements, procedures, contact personnel, account numbers, pin numbers, and access codes.

- **Access.** In a dire emergency, you can access your funds from an IRA without any lengthy approval process or delay. (Of course, you may be subject to taxes and penalty tax for premature withdrawal.)

- **Financial Advice.** Most retirement plans won't offer specific financial advice. As the balances grow, you may find that you require professional advice to combine your IRAs and personal accounts into a comprehensive investment plan.

Accomplishing the Rollover

It's important to avoid any receipt of the funds that might trigger an unanticipated tax consequence. The "trustee-to-trustee" transfer prevents any possibility of a taxable event occurring during the transfer process. (If you do decide to hire an investment advisor, the advisor assists you in completing the process.)

Open an account with the financial institution of your choice. You should consider a discount brokerage like TD Waterhouse or Fidelity to maximize your investment choices, but you might want to use a large, no-load fund family like Vanguard.

After the account is opened, give the account number and complete address to your old pension administrator or HR department. Instruct them to send the proceeds directly to the new custodian.

In the event that you made non–tax-deductible contributions to the old plan, the administrator sends you a separate check for the amount of your contributions. That check should be made out to you—it cannot be rolled over into an IRA. However, the growth on your contributions can be. Consider investing the check for your contributions in funds that generate low turnover and tax liabilities—for instance, a total market index fund.

When the funds have arrived at the new custodian, invest them to meet your long-term retirement needs.

Expect a form 1099R from your old plan. Hold on to it. Even though you don't have a taxable event, you need to show the rollover on your next annual tax return.

Lesson 24 ———————————

At Age 50, the Catch-Up Provisions

At age 50, you can make additional contributions to your IRAs, 401(k), 403(b), and 457 plans. These additional contributions were designed to help folks who are not on track for a comfortable retirement to "catch up." But everyone should take advantage of the additional tax-sheltered savings opportunities if they have access to a decent qualified plan, or if they can make IRA contributions.

Contribution limits for 401(k), 403(b), and 457 plans increase by $5,000 a year at age 50, and IRA contribution limits increase by an additional $1,000 for both Roth and Regular IRAs. Take advantage of this free gift from Uncle Sam to boost your retirement savings.

Lesson 25 ─────────────────

Approaching Retirement
Transition Planning

It would be a mistake to wait until the last possible moment to change strategies from accumulation to distribution. The investor will want to transition from the full accumulation mode to the retirement asset allocation plan sometime in advance of retirement date in order to assure that sufficient liquidity is available when needed.

After all, you wouldn't want your retirement tomorrow dependent on what the market did today. If you are not properly positioned in advance, a couple of bad years in the market might set back your retirement date a decade or more. An orderly migration strategy from accumulation to distribution strategies ensures that you won't be hung out to dry if the market turns south. By gradually reducing equity exposure until the desired portfolio is reached sometime before retirement, the glide slope approach, explained later, handles this problem quite neatly by systematically reducing your equity exposure as you near your target retirement date.

Of course, if stocks earn more than bonds during the transition period, you will have a somewhat smaller nest egg. Economists call that potential underperformance an opportunity cost. But, you have greatly reduced the chance that a possible market crash will leave you unable to retire at all. So, the opportunity cost might be a small price to pay for peace of mind.

An investment strategy isn't necessarily about maximizing returns while ignoring risk. Most often, the appropriate strategy is the one that maximizes the probability of a successful outcome. That requires considering both risk and return. Migrating early to your preferred retirement portfolio greatly increases your chance of a successful retirement experience.

See the next lesson for more on investment tactics as you approach retirement.

Lesson 26 ─────────────────────────

Early Retirement Tactics:
How to Avoid the Tax Traps

If you have the necessary capital, taxes shouldn't prevent you from retiring early. A little planning will avoid those pesky penalties.

How to Retire Early and Not Pay the Taxman a Penalty

So you want to retire early? Good for you. But, even if you have enough total funds to support yourself comfortably, some retirement plan assets may be locked away or awkward to access.

By now, almost everyone is aware of the 10% penalty imposed on early withdrawals from qualified retirement plans. These are imposed, subject to a few exceptions (such as death, disability, education expense, or first-time home purchase), on any distribution prior to age $59\frac{1}{2}$.

Exceptions to the Early Distribution Tax Penalties

You do not have to pay the additional 10% tax penalty on your early retirement distribution if you meet the criteria of certain exceptions.

The following are the exceptions for early distributions from an IRA:

- You were permanently or totally disabled.
- You were unemployed and paid for health insurance premiums.
- You paid for college expenses for yourself or a dependent.
- You bought a house.[1]
- You paid for medical expenses exceeding 7.5% of your adjusted gross income.
- The IRS levied your retirement account to pay off tax debts.

The following are exceptions for early distributions from a qualified retirement plan, such as a 401(k) or 403(b) plan:

- Distributions upon the death or disability of the plan participant.
- You were age 55 or over and you retired or left your job.
- You received the distribution as part of "substantially equal payments" over your lifetime.
- You paid for medical expenses exceeding 7.5% of your adjusted gross income.
- The distributions were required by a divorce decree or separation agreement ("qualified domestic relations court order").
- You had a "direct rollover" to your new retirement account.
- You received a lump-sum payment but rolled over the money to a qualified retirement account within 60 days.

To avoid the penalty, try to live off your personal accounts until you are past the age 59½ early retirement penalty tax period. This maximizes deferral, avoids potential tax penalties for early retirement, and provides the greatest flexibility.

---

[1] The home-buying exception has the following additional restrictions: You did not own a home in the previous two years, and only $10,000 of the retirement distribution qualifies to avoid the tax penalty but not the ordinary income tax.

However, if you don't have sufficient personal assets to provide for your income needs until age 59½, and you don't qualify for one of the preceding exceptions, all is not lost. There are three provisions you should know about, as follows:

1. If you have money in a 401(k) or other qualified retirement plan, and your employer permits it, you may be able to withdraw assets without penalty if you separated from service after age 55. This might be a great source of funds if you retire between 55 and 59½. Note: Not all qualified plans allow this; it depends on the plan document. This distribution option is not available to IRAs.

2. If you have employer stock at a low basis inside your retirement plan, there is a little-known provision that might be very valuable to you. You can withdraw your employer stock from the plan paying tax only on your basis. If you sell the stock immediately, the profit is subject to capital gains rates. This provision may allow you to transfer a significant value out of your plan at very favorable tax rates. By systematically liquidating your company stock over the number of years until age 59½, you might be able to support yourself at very low total tax cost.

Do-It-Yourself

www.Sink-Swim.com

Company Stock Distribution Analysis Calculator: If you own company stock in a retirement plan, you might be able to take advantage of using the long-term capital gains tax rate rather than your ordinary income tax rate on this investment.

Keep in mind that the special provision for company stock must be part of a total distribution from the plan, and you may not pick and choose shares at other than the average cost basis of the stock. The balance of the distribution might be rolled over into an IRA just like any other total distribution. However, if you roll over the stock into an IRA, the option is lost.

3. Finally, if you have not reached age 59½, you still can tap into your retirement plan assets under a plan of "substantially equal distributions over your projected lifetime" under an IRS regulation commonly referred to as Section 72(t). You are required to continue your distributions until the later of age 59½ or five years. Any deviations subject you to 10% penalties on all previous distributions. So, it's definitely not flexible.

The regulations give us three ways to calculate allowable withdrawals. Between them, you can design almost any reasonable schedule of distributions. Starting from the smallest distributions, they are as follows:

- Divide your life expectancy or the joint life expectancy (from the IRS tables of you and your beneficiary) into the balance of your account on December 31 of the previous year.

- Amortize your account over your life expectancy or your joint life expectancy with your beneficiary using a "reasonable" interest rate. Use an annuity factor derived from the IRS tables for your life expectancy or the joint life expectancy of you and your beneficiary.

Do-It-Yourself

www.Sink-Swim.com

72(t) Calculator: The IRS Rule 72(t) allows for penalty-free early withdrawals from retirement accounts. Use this calculator to determine your allowable 72(t) distribution and how it can help fund your early retirement.

72(t) Distribution Impact: This calculator is designed to examine the affects of 72(t) distributions on your retirement plan balance.

IRS Pub 590 gives you detailed instructions and all the tables referred to previously.

If your calculated distribution is more than you think you need, you can split your IRA into smaller accounts that give you the distribution you want. Later, if you need to, you can begin another distribution from another IRA. But each separate distribution starts the clock running for its own five-year period.

Coming Soon to a Seminar Near You...Retirement Part 59½

When it comes to retirement and living off your nest egg, 59½ is the magic age because you are finally old enough to take cookies (money) out of the retirement cookie jar (IRA or other qualified account) without your mother (the IRS) spanking your hand and charging you a 10% tax penalty. Not coincidentally, 59½ is around the age when people retire, and brokers know it. As a result, they put the full court press on marketing to consumers around this age, hoping to catch big accounts from 401(k) and other retirement plan rollovers. If you are in your fifties or older, you probably receive invitations on a weekly basis from financial "professionals" inviting you to attend "free" seminars that typically include a steak dinner or, if you are a seafood lover, the Hungry Boy Seafood Platter.

If you attend these seminars simply for the free food and do not plan to invest, my only advice is to make sure you bring the Rolaids. If, however, you are considering retiring younger than 59½ and plan to make withdrawals from your 401(k) or qualified account, you need to be aware of how section §72(t) of the IRS code operates because you could be setting yourself up for a disaster.

Some of the most heart-wrenching cases involve early retirees who get into trouble with §72(t). Don't become a victim! For example, a group of retirees in their early 50s were induced into cashing in their pension and living off the proceeds. The broker promised that they could easily withdraw 12 percent per year with no risk of ever running out of money. Of course, they ran out of money in less than five years, but the really bad part of the story was that they were doomed from the start because of 72(t). Remember, to avoid paying the 10% tax penalty, you have to commit to a certain withdrawal rate for 5 years or 59½, whichever is longer. In one instance, my client was 52 at the time she made the first systematic withdrawal at a rate of 14%. Therefore, she was locked to make those withdrawals until she turned 59½, which was 7½ years away. By committing to this high withdrawal rate, she was in essence betting that her investments were going to grow more than 14% per year for 7½ years. Ludicrous! To make matters worse, the 14% withdrawal rate exceeded what the IRS determined to be "reasonable," and she could have been liable to the IRS on that basis alone.

Of course, the broker who talked my client into doing this never explained it to her in this way. Why? Because he was selling her something. Had the broker explained these risks, she probably wouldn't have done it.

—Contributed by Jason Doss

Conclusion

If you have enough capital to retire, the various tax and pension regulations will not provide much of an obstacle. With just a little advanced planning, you will soon be sailing off into the sunset.

Lesson 27

70 is the New 65:
Delayed Retirement Advantages

If you're approaching 65 and don't have enough salted away to meet your goals, all is not lost. Consider that by delaying retirement just a few years, you could be living on easy street.

Somewhere in a parallel universe, everyone reaches their target retirement date with plenty of funds to see them safely through the rest of their lives. No one ever gets divorced, works for a company without a retirement plan, is forced into early retirement, makes poor investments, sends three children to graduate school, delays saving for retirement, saves too little or not at all, or gets wiped out by major medical expense. But we live in this universe, and here "stuff happens."

We have all seen the dreary statistics: Millions of boomers are heading off into their sunset retirement years with too few resources. The country has a zero net savings. Traditional retirement plans cover fewer people each year, and many have failed outright.

In the first place, there's nothing magic about age 65. No one says you must retire on that date. It was selected as the target retirement age in Germany in 1889 by Chancellor Otto von Bismarck when he created the world's first Social Security system. It was chosen in part because only a very few people were going to live long enough to qualify for benefits. As an added bonus, even if they did live to 65, they could be expected to die before receiving much in the way of payments.

One hundred years ago, age 65 was considered older than dirt. Not so today where many people feel that they are just hitting their stride at 65. Nevertheless, the idea that 65 was the appropriate retirement age stuck in peoples' minds in spite of the fact that 65 is a completely arbitrary number.

Today, with modern medicine and better living conditions, people live a whole lot longer. Instead of planning on being dead at 65, you have to plan to support yourself until at least age 95 and, perhaps, longer. Living that long requires a lot of financial assets. But many boomers, for a number of reasons, are unprepared as they approach retirement.

What benefits might you derive if you push back retirement to age 70? First, let's talk about the non-economic reasons:

- **You are still having fun at work.** There are lots of people who can't imagine leaving something they enjoy. Spending the rest of their lives rocking on the front porch is just not where they want to be.

- **It's time for a second career.** You may not make as much as you once did, but you may avoid having to tap your retirement assets. Perhaps you have always wanted to start a bed and breakfast in Maine, lecture at your local college, or write the great American novel. You might consult in your field, teach English in Shanghai, or even join the Peace Corps.

- **You want to work fewer hours and reduce stress.** You could go part-time, or take a less stressful position. This keeps you "in the game," but gives you time for other activities and the chance to kick back a little, relax, and smell the flowers. Again, you might not make as much, but you won't have to tap into the retirement nest egg.

If your motives are economic—in other words, if your nest egg isn't quite grand enough to support you in the style to which you aspire—then pushing back your date a few years can yield dramatic benefits, as follows:

- Your existing savings can grow for an additional five years. Let's say you reach age 65 with a nest egg of $500,000. At a "safe" 4% withdrawal rate, that's only $20,000 a year. But if you defer retirement for five years and have an average growth rate of 8% on your funds, that nest egg grows to $734,664. At that same, safe withdrawal rate, you can take out $36,733 a year. That's 47% more income.

- You can save and invest during those additional years. $20,000 a year for five years, invested at a net of 8%, grows to an additional $117,332. Adding that to your enhanced, age-70 nest egg grows the account to $851,996, yielding a total annual income of $34,079. That's a lot better than the $20,000 a year you might have had at age 65.

- You will have fewer years left in which to spend the dollars, which might allow you to take a higher withdrawal rate without fear of running out of money. After looking at the other facts surrounding your financial situation, you might feel that a slightly higher withdrawal rate is safe. Suppose you selected 4.5% instead of the 4% we started with. That bumps your annual retirement income to $38,940.

- Your Social Security goes up every month that you delay after your "normal" retirement date. If you retire at 65, a quick check on the Social Security System Web Site Calculator (www.ssa.gov/planners/calculators.htm) shows the benefit to be $2,005 a month. But, if you wait until age 70, it rises to $2,929. That's 46% more! There is no additional benefit past age 70.

Do-It-Yourself

www.Sink-Swim.com

Social Security Benefits: Use this calculator to estimate your Social Security benefits.

How Important Is Social Security? Use this calculator to determine how losing this important retirement asset could affect you.

- Your defined benefit, profit sharing, 403(b), and 401(k) plans will benefit from increased contributions and/or investment returns.

- If you are fortunate enough to be covered by a defined benefit pension plan, your benefits will increase a great deal with another five years of service and potentially higher terminal pay plugged into the benefit formula. Annuity rates are increased for older retirees because, on average, the plan will have to pay out fewer years. So, you might benefit from three enhancements to your defined benefit formula: higher salary, more years in the compensation formula, and better annuity rates.

  Even if you quit work, but delay receiving benefits from your defined benefit pension plan until 70, the fund goes on increasing in value, and the annuity rates improve. This alone might improve your benefits by as much as 50%. (Annuity rates, service credits, and assumed investment returns vary widely from plan to plan. Consult your summary plan description or check with your HR department.)

Summary

Nobody ever said that each of us had to retire at 65. Delaying retirement by just a few years can enhance benefits substantially, turning the prospect of a threadbare existence into one of abundance and security.

Taxation Without Representation

You probably don't know this, but most brokerage firms prohibit their brokers from giving tax advice. Yet, in reality, it is frequently impossible for the broker to make a recommendation to you without giving tax advice. For example, if a broker recommends that you sell your company stock held in your 401(k) and invest the proceeds in a non-qualified account, common sense tells you that the broker gave you bad tax advice because you will have to pay income taxes—possibly with a penalty—because you didn't roll the money into another qualified account, right? From a legal standpoint...absolutely. From a practical standpoint...not so fast.

Let me clue you into how this story frequently ends. The brokerage firm and the broker will likely deny that tax advice was ever given and, if you sue, the issue will be minimized to a he-said, she-said dispute. If you happen to use a CPA to do your taxes, they point to the CPA. If you don't use a CPA, the brokerage firm might point the finger at you and say that you came up with the idea.

From a cost perspective, even though the out-of-pocket losses may be a lot of money to you, it may not be enough to warrant filing a lawsuit over. For these reasons, you are better off avoiding the problem in the first place. Should this type of issue occur, ask the brokers to explain the tax implications of the recommendation. If they agree, make them explain it to you in writing. If they refuse, then you know where you stand on that issue, and you can evaluate whether to rely on their recommendation at all.

—Contributed by Jason Doss

Lesson 28

At Retirement

Few subjects provoke as much emotional stress as the later stages of retirement planning. Our jobs and money both become part of our self-image. Suddenly, both seem at risk. Our nest egg has to last forever, while providing us with liquid income. Quite a trick.

Investment tactics during retirement require a balance between liquidity and growth. The right balance is so important that an entire lesson is devoted to it Lessons 36 to 40 in Part V, "Investing to Meet Your Goals."

Critical Choice: Lump Sum Versus Annuity for Distributions

Annuity Options for DB Plans—How to Decide

The standard option for a defined benefit (DB) plan is a joint and one half survivor annuity, according to which you take a reduced annuity for the rest of your life and half the remaining benefit goes to your spouse upon your death.

Do-It-Yourself

www.Sink-Swim.com

Pension Plan Retirement Options: Use this calculator to help decide between joint survivorship and single survivorship pension options.

But, there may be better options for your family. The annuity feature has a cost associated with it that your family may or may not need. For instance, if the employee is in great health and the spouse is in very bad health, the family might be better off to waive the annuity and purchase insurance to provide for the spouse. Conversely, if the employee is in very bad health, the family might opt for a 100% survivor annuity.

Lump Sum or Annuity

DB plans are designed so that on retirement date, the plan provides an annuity to provide the lifetime income benefit. But, some plans allow participants to opt for a lump-sum payment, which shifts the responsibility for investments to the retiree. The trade-off is that the lump sum creates an estate that can be passed on to heirs, and the possibility of potentially higher income or inflation protection.

Choosing the right option must start with a realistic comparison between the guaranteed income under the plan and the income that can be generated under a sustainable withdrawal rate. If the plan is offering a guaranteed $8,000 a year or a lump sum of $100,000, it's unlikely that your investment acumen can equal the annuity because 6% is at the very top end of the scale of sustainable withdrawal rates, and 4% to 5% is a more comfortable assumption.

There are other factors that might influence your decision. For instance, if your health is poor, your family might be better off with the lump sum. If the company is in financial difficulty and there is a chance the plan might be terminated in distress, the option to take the money and run becomes more attractive. This is especially true if your benefit level is in excess of the PBGC insurance amount.

Defined Benefit with a Lump-Sum Option

As more and more people reach the age where they contemplate (or dream of) early retirement, more and more unscrupulous investment salespeople come out of the woodwork to take advantage of that dream. "Wannabe" retirees are often targeted in large numbers at employer-sponsored events, retirement parties, and similar gatherings.

Brokers bait the hook by asserting very firmly that by following their advice, attendees in their 40s and 50s with savings of no more than several hundred thousand dollars can experience an enjoyable retirement by taking a lump sum distribution of their pension savings and following the broker's investment recommendations. Retirees are told that their investment returns will duplicate their lost wages and that they can live off the returns without ever touching the principle. The broker often cites an average return generated by the stock market over a period of time, showing them charts and graphs depicting such returns.

I have represented a number of clients who were in their early 50s when they left their stable jobs of 30 years and cashed in their pensions based on the false promise by a broker that they could make more money in retirement than while working. Five years later, these "retirees" are in their mid-50s and their entire pensions are gone! The market went down while they were withdrawing monthly income to survive. Getting a new job at the age of 55 with nothing more than a high school diploma is virtually impossible. Your only options may be mowing grass or working as a Wal-Mart greeter. When sued, the brokerage firm's main defense is that it was your idea to retire and that you are entirely to blame because you spent the money. Although these are very good lawsuits to bring, they are, at the same time, very sad.

Most experts advise you not to withdraw more than 4% of your principle in any single year if you hope not to run out of money before you die. But brokers who make this type of sales pitch often assure you that you can withdraw 8%, 10%, or 12% every year with no problem and no risk of running out of money. If you hear such a pitch, run (don't walk) for the exit. It is a lie. Why would they lie?

Because it is the only way to convince you as a prospective client that you can "earn" enough in retirement to replace your wages and, thus, the only way the broker can gather your assets. Gathering assets is what the "retirement seminar" is really all about. Attendees believe the seminar is about them and their retirements. No, it's not about you. The name of the game is gathering assets and how the broker makes money.

If you have a DB plan, my only advice is to think long and hard before taking the lump-sum option. Compare your options carefully. Under the traditional pension options, your guaranteed monthly income generally stops upon your death. If your company goes belly up before you die, you may be out of luck. On the other hand, the main benefit of the lump-sum option is that you are in control of your own money and that you can leave money to your heirs.

If you worked for a large company like GE or AT&T and are really not that concerned about the company's long survival, your primary motivation for considering the lump-sum option is probably that you want to leave money to your children. If that is the case, simply calculate how much money you would receive per month by withdrawing 4% per year and compare it to how much you would receive per month under the traditional pension option. If you can live off 4% per year in withdrawals, then good for you. If you can't and need more monthly income to live, understand that with every additional percent in withdrawals, you expose your portfolio to more risk.

Your common sense will tell you that, if you lived paycheck to paycheck for your entire career, you should probably stick with the traditional pension option and not take the lump sum. I have seen too many clients unable to handle the responsibility of managing a seemingly large lump sum of money. The temptation to overspend is too great.

—*Contributed by Jason Doss*

Which Assets to Spend First During Retirement?

This section discusses why maintaining your tax benefits as long as possible makes you wealthier, and when to break that rule.

Many investors arrive at retirement with several different classes of assets. For instance, you might hold non-qualified deferred compensation plans, 401(k)s, IRAs, Roth IRAs, non-qualified annuities, and taxable investment accounts.

Does it make any difference which you spend first? You bet! The tax treatment varies widely between types of accounts. Therefore, determining the pecking order for withdrawals will have important implications.

Retirement is a very good time to review your entire financial plan to insure that the investments match the new financial situation. These decisions must not be made in a vacuum.

As you already know, all other things are rarely equal. The various kinds of accounts may have differing or severely limited investment choices. For instance, a 401(k) plan may be heavily weighted with employer stock, or the plan might offer only expensive annuities. Retirees might not have total control over the timing and form of payment for many assets. Finally, a retiree might hold highly concentrated positions in company stock or options requiring sophisticated analysis and strategy. Retirement offers a chance to rationalize all these assets by freeing them up for more effective deployment.

No two retirees have identical situations or objectives. But, here are some considerations and guidelines that might help you to prioritize your withdrawals.

As a rule of thumb, try to retain the assets with the best tax attributes. During your lifetime, you will be wealthier if you defer taxes on your tax-qualified retirement plans as long as possible. So, consider liquidating personal accounts first before you tap into the qualified money.

There is at least one exception to the preceding rule of thumb. If estate considerations are more important to you than current or lifetime income, you might want to draw down IRAs and other retirement plan assets before your stock accounts so that the stocks can receive a "step up in basis" at your death. This means that the capital gains are forgiven, and your heirs take the assets free from any capital gains tax obligations as of the date of death. This assumes that you are wealthy enough so that you don't really need the retirement assets. Regular IRAs are taxed in your estate and the beneficiaries must pay income tax as the proceeds are withdrawn, diminishing the value to them when compared to appreciated stock accounts.

In all cases, if you have Roth IRA accounts, use them last. Roth accounts have the most favorable tax treatment both while you are alive and in your estate.

Early Retirees

If possible, try to live off your personal accounts until at least past the age 59½ early retirement penalty tax period. This maximizes deferral, avoids potential tax penalties for early retirement, and provides the greatest flexibility. For instance, consider liquidating any company stock, exercising stock options, and draw down non-qualified deferred compensation. Then liquidate your general brokerage accounts.

Normal Retirees

Even though you are not faced with early withdrawal penalties, you will want to pursue the same strategy. Use your private taxable accounts first in order to maximize the benefits of tax deferral. Of course, you need to keep enough cash on hand to handle emergencies.

Required Minimum Distributions (RMD) at Age 70½

Beginning at age 70½, the IRS demands that you begin to disburse all those funds that they never got to tax. The calculation that determines how much you must take out is very simple. They assume that the beneficiary is 10 years younger than the account holder. Then they divide life expectancy into the previous year-end account balance to determine the Required Minimum Distribution (RMD). In the event the beneficiary is a spouse more than ten years younger than the account holder, they use the beneficiary's actual age to determine life expectancy. Otherwise, everybody uses the same table, conveniently found in IRS Pub 590.

Do-It-Yourself

www.Sink-Swim.com

Required Minimum Distribution (RMD): Use this calculator to determine your Required Minimum Distribution (RMD) as an account owner of a retirement account. This financial calculator also looks at potential future year's distribution requirements.

Early in the program, required distributions are not large. With luck, your account is growing faster than the RMD. But as you age, your life expectancy goes down, and so the required distributions increase. RMDs never reach 100%, but larger distributions eventually deplete the account. For instance, at age 70½, your RMD is only 3.6%; at 80, it climbs to 5.3%. By age 90, though, the RMD is 8.7%. The IRS thoughtfully provides values through age 110.

Summary

As guidelines, most investors will want to liquidate assets during retirement in the following order:

- Personal taxable accounts, including non-qualified deferred compensation plans and company stock accounts
- Regular IRAs, other qualified pension plans, and non-qualified annuities
- Roth IRAs

Paying Off the House at Retirement

Financial leverage issues boil down to a very simple premise: You're going to borrow money to buy an asset that will grow faster than the cost of servicing the debt. Optimistic investors will leverage their accounts by buying stocks on margin in the hopes of increasing their return on capital. Hedge funds use leverage to boost their returns, often using derivatives to run up leverage far in excess of what mere margin might provide.

Another use of leverage is to acquire assets that you can't afford to pay cash for or don't want to pay off immediately. For instance, businesses borrow money to build factories. They expect that their income from manufacturing will pay off the debt over time.

The techniques are sure-fire as long as the asset performs at or above expectations, and the level of debt payments doesn't mushroom. But, neither one of these assumptions has to come true. If it doesn't, then risk, the ugly twin-side of increased return, bites you.

Leverage amplifies both risk and potential return. In a simple example, an investor puts down $20,000 and buys a $100,000 real estate property. If the property increases in value to $120,000, the investor now has $40,000 of equity and has earned a 100% profit on his initial $20,000 contribution. But, suppose the property value falls to $80,000? Now the investor has zero equity and has lost his entire investment. A huge number of real estate speculators are in the process of learning that painful lesson. Investors often underestimate the risk of real estate.

Do-It-Yourself

www.Sink-Swim.com

Investment Loan: This calculator helps illustrate the effect of using a loan to purchase an investment or appreciable asset. Using debt as leverage to purchase investments can magnify your return. The downside is that you also increase your risk.

Most homeowners are motivated not so much for profit as to enjoy the use of a property that they can't necessarily afford to pay off at closing. Unless you bought very recently, you, as a homeowner, probably have seen increases in value that have built up substantial equity. You might have stretched to buy your house a number of years ago, but now see the payment as very affordable. At retirement, you might have the assets to pay off the mortgage, but wonder if that is a smart thing to do.

In the spirit of full disclosure, let me start by acknowledging a non-trivial conflict of interest. As an advisor who charges a fee based on assets under management, if you withdraw your funds from our accounts, my firm generates less income.

The answer to whether you should pay off the mortgage depends on how comfortable you are with financial leverage and how much leverage you are willing and financially able to bear.

The argument for keeping the mortgage is that the after-tax cost of servicing the debt can be very low. For instance, if your mortgage is fixed at 6% and you are in the 33% tax bracket, the after-tax cost is only 4% because you are deducting interest payments on your home against your taxes. You may feel that you can invest for a higher after-tax return somewhere else. If you are fortunate to have gobs and gobs of cash flow in excess of your needs, this might be a good trade-off. Over the long run, you could very well end up wealthier. Even if that's the case, make sure you are comfortable with the risk and understand the trade-offs.

The argument for paying off the mortgage is that it eliminates a monthly expense that must be paid even if the value of the house goes down at the same time that the other investment goes down. The situation is even worse if you don't have a fixed mortgage and interest charges or other charges go up. The newspapers are full of stories of homeowners who took that gamble and lost. If your financial situation is precarious, and you are living paycheck to paycheck or close to your retirement income, that may be an intolerable risk.

The only time that paying off the mortgage is a bad choice is when the assets come out of a qualified plan or IRA. Depending on your state, local, and federal tax bite, you might have to liquidate $150,000 of assets or more to pay off a $100,000 mortgage. I don't think that trade-off makes good economic sense. You would be giving up the advantages of your mortgage deduction on one side and, on the other side, you would be giving up the qualified plan's deferral value and accelerating taxes.

On the other hand, you might ask the reverse question: Should you mortgage the house to invest more in the stock market? Not surprisingly, that question comes up most often after a couple of good years in the market. The temptation is to "free up" some of that "trapped" home equity. However, it is certain that somewhere, there is a homeowner with no other debt, lots of excess cash flow, and a healthy appetite for risk that might come to another conclusion. But, for most of us, retirement is not the time to leverage up our risk profile.

Additional Considerations

Estate Planning

Many retirees want to ensure that their assets, including retirement plans, will not be consumed by unnecessary costs and transfer taxes. With proper planning, a beneficiary may be able to defer income tax for many more years on the vast majority of an inherited IRA. Appropriate attention must be paid to beneficiary selection of qualified plans and coordination with a comprehensive estate plan. Roth IRA conversion may be the most powerful, overlooked, and under-used estate-planning opportunity available for many retirees.

Do-It-Yourself

www.Sink-Swim.com

Roth IRA Conversion: This calculator will show the advantage, if any, of converting your IRA to a Roth.

Use of various and properly designed estate planning documents (such as trusts, durable powers of attorney, health care designations, and so on) may minimize potential estate taxes, reduce probate fees and expenses, and provide a management tool in the event of incapacity.

See the "Web Extra" section on estate planning with retirement plan assets at www.Sink-Swim.com.

Bad Financial Advice and What You Might Do About It

As explained earlier, asset allocation is the key to a well-managed portfolio. All well-managed portfolios have a diversified mix of different investment classes, such as cash, stocks, and bonds. Liquidity is also important because, should something go wrong in the short-term, you need to be able to convert some or all of your portfolio into cash without paying too high a price. Your broker has a duty to ensure that your account has this capability.

Many of my clients involve retirees who depend on their investments for monthly income. Some examples of income-producing investments include CDs, bonds, stocks that pay dividends, and income-producing mutual funds. Most of my clients who get into trouble are those who need income but also need growth because they do not have enough money to invest in the first place. Brokers frequently recommend that clients in this situation invest their money in non–income-producing growth investments such as growth mutual funds. The hope is that the investments will grow at high enough rates so that they can be sold to create income. This is financial suicide!

Rather than just being brutally candid with the customers, brokers commonly sugarcoat the truth and fail to explain just how risky the strategy is. Why? Because a good sales pitch focuses on rewards, not risks. Brokers have a duty to explain all risks associated with their recommendations, and they can be held liable should something go wrong (and in this strategy, something will go wrong).

I once successfully represented a retired CPA who hired a young, attractive, inexperienced female broker to manage his retirement assets. Prior to meeting her, he had only ever invested in six-month CDs for his monthly income. However, interest rates on CDs were low at that time, and he was looking for other low-risk, income-producing investments that paid slightly better returns.

What did she recommend? A variable annuity with a nine-year surrender charge penalty period. (Cashing in the contract before the end of the surrender period results in a hefty penalty.) Outrageous, but very common. There was no explanation for her recommendation other than that she got paid a handsome 7% commission. Other, more appropriate investments available at that time paid only 1%–2% commissions. Of course she recommended the annuity. To make matters worse, she recommended that he invest all the money inside the annuity in non–income-producing, technology-based mutual funds. What a great idea…NOT!

The product was sold in March 2000; the very next month, the technology bubble burst, and the client lost more than half of his nest egg between 2000 and 2003. During that time, he experienced what I like to call the "deer in the headlights" method of investing. He would call and complain to his broker about the market losses, and she would always encourage him to stay the course and tell him that the market would come back. The client and the broker knew that if he surrendered the annuity, he would automatically lose 10% of money due to the surrender charge. Even though my client was a very smart man and was a CPA, all of this caused him to freeze because he was caught between a rock and a hard place. Just because you are a CPA doesn't mean you know the first thing about investing.

Luckily, an arbitration panel awarded him most of his money back from the brokerage firm, but the lesson was hard on him and his family. He called frequently to say how guilty he felt for exposing his family to hardship.

—*Contributed by Jason Doss*

Three Common Claims Brought by Investors

Unsuitability

Brokers often make recommendations to purchase or sell a particular security. Investment decisions should be made only in light of the goals and needs of the investor. That is why the law imposes a duty on brokers to recommend only securities that the broker reasonably believes are suitable for the investor. The broker's belief must be based upon a reasonable inquiry concerning the customer's investment objectives, financial situation and needs, tax status, other security holdings, and any other relevant information known by the broker.

An unsuitable recommendation of securities constitutes a dishonest, unethical, and fraudulent business practice. If such a recommendation results in financial loss, the customer has a right to recover that loss from the individual broker and the brokerage firm. Nevertheless, unsuitable recommendations of securities are among the most common violations in the brokerage industry.

An investment might be unsuitable if it is inconsistent with the customer's investment objectives. For example, if an investor needs to withdraw money from investments to meet living expenses, the broker should not recommend investments that tend to fluctuate significantly in value and pay little or no dividends, such as growth stocks. If the money is a "rainy day" fund that might need to be tapped for unexpected expenses, the broker should not recommend a long-term, illiquid investment like a variable annuity, which imposes significant surrender charges on withdrawals over a pre-determined amount. If the money being invested constitutes a significant portion of the customer's net worth, or if the customer's risk tolerance is low, the broker should not recommend that a significant portion of that money be placed in investments with above-average risk characteristics, such as a small cap or international stocks. These are just a few examples of why certain investments might flunk the suitability test.

Benchmarks for determining whether an investment or investment portfolio is suitable include the investor's objective(s), time horizon, and risk tolerance. To protect yourself, you should send your broker a statement of your investment objectives, time horizon, and risk tolerance at least annually, and have your account reviewed periodically by an attorney experienced in securities arbitration.

Churning

Brokerage accounts are sometimes described as being "churned and burned." *Churning* refers to the excessive buying and selling of securities in your account by your broker for the purpose of generating commissions. Although active trading may be suitable in rare instances, churning, by definition, is always unsuitable. Churning can decimate an account. If you see a lot of buying and selling in your account that you did not specifically intend to be an actively traded, high-risk account, you should consult with an attorney experienced in securities arbitration.

Unauthorized Trading

Unsuitability and churning are forms of fraud. So is unauthorized trading. Unauthorized trading occurs when your broker buys or sells a security in your account without your prior approval. Unless you sign a formal agreement giving your broker permission to manage your account without seeking prior approval for each transaction, your broker must make sure that you approve each transaction before it happens.

Unauthorized trading occurs most often in firms where there is a large incentive for the broker to meet commission goals, or quotas. Some firms, for example, have sales contests in which brokers who generate a certain amount of business receive expensive trips or other prizes. In other circumstances, personal financial problems may motivate a broker to trade and generate commissions without your permission.

What Do You Do When You Suspect That You Have Been Victimized?

Ideally, no one will ever be a victim of investment abuse. But what happens if you become a victim? How should you handle it?

The biggest mistake that investors make is that in the heat of passion, they write a nasty letter to the broker or, better yet, to state regulators. That will show them, right? Wrong.

Although writing a letter might make you feel better in the short term, the words that you write down are memorialized forever, and they might come back to haunt you should you ever have to file a lawsuit. There are two very important lessons about dealing with clients in financial trouble.

First, because a violation of trust is involved, victims commonly blame themselves. They are often embarrassed and feel guilty for exposing their families to financial hardship. As a result, the victim's brain immediately begins to replay details of every meeting that ever took place with the broker in an attempt to reconstruct the series of events that led to the problem. When clients come into the office, there are commonly heard statements like, "I knew that guy was a crook at our first meeting." Someone immediately corrects the client by saying, "No, you didn't. No rational person would ever invest their money with someone whom they knew to be a crook."

The bottom line is that a victim's memory is flawed because it creates memories that never occurred and incorrectly assigns blame as a coping mechanism.

Statements such as, "I knew that guy was a crook at our first meeting…" always tend to find their way to the complaint letter and can really sink your case should a lawsuit ever get filed.

Secondly, most clients only discover that they were victims of investment abuse or improper advice when their monthly statements show investment losses. The investor does not understand why the investments went down or, more importantly, how the losses could have been avoided.

Despite not knowing why the investments went south, the victim will write in the complaint letter something like, "I told him that I wanted my money to grow." Because you wrote down the word "grow," the brokerage firm's lawyers will try to paint you as a risky investor even when you are not.

Clients are always discouraged from writing complaint letters, especially when angry. Instead, they are told to capitalize on the anger by beginning to draft a personal chronology of events, which forces the client to articulate the sequence of events. It is a living document because information can be added over time. You may see something on TV months later that reminds you of something the broker told you during a meeting such as, "I guarantee this investment will grow 12% every year."

People who think they have been victimized are also urged to speak to a lawyer who specializes in securities arbitrations. Attorneys are typically good writers and, more importantly, they are not emotionally involved. Securities arbitration lawyers also are familiar with the dynamics of the customer-broker relationship and the types of investments in your accounts. A good securities arbitration attorney will also be able to tell you why the investments were inappropriate for you and how the losses could have been avoided.

The Arbitration

You may not have noticed it when you first opened your brokerage account. It was very small. You probably needed a magnifying glass to read it, but its consequences are huge. What am I referring to? Pre-dispute arbitration clauses contained in the customer agreement with your brokerage firm.

These sneaky little clauses are buried in the fine print of virtually every brokerage firm customer agreement, and they become very important when something goes wrong between you and your broker. Pre-dispute arbitration clauses require customers to waive their right to a jury trial and to resolve any and all disputes with the firm or the financial advisor in arbitration. These provisions are commonly contained in the customer agreement you signed when you first opened your brokerage account.

Arbitration is very different from a court proceeding. The trials are typically held at hotels instead of courtrooms. There is no judge and no jury deciding your case. Instead, a panel of three individuals acts as the judge and jury. The trials are held in secret and, even worse, one of the panel members is required to be a person who currently works in the brokerage industry.

Skeptics of the process insist that arbitrations are unfair to consumers and portray the industry arbitrator as "Big Brother" to protect fellow brokers from liability. Supporters argue that arbitration is the most cost-effective way to resolve these disputes. Regardless of what side you are on, statistics show that customers win only about half the time and, even when they do, are generally awarded only a fraction of their losses.

If you have ever been a claimant in an arbitration proceeding, you know that when sued, the brokerage firms deny...deny...deny that they owed you any duty at all. All the trust built up between you and your broker is thrown out the window by the brokerage firm, and the scope of the once-clear trust relationship is reduced to a he-said, she-said dispute between you and the broker.

You are much better off avoiding such problems altogether. The key to avoiding pitfalls is self-education. Don't rely on the paramedic to save you from drowning. You are better off learning to be a good swimmer.

Despite all the negatives of arbitration, if you find yourself in a dispute with a financial professional or their firm, all is not lost. The important thing to remember is that you are not totally to blame for the tragic circumstances. You simply trusted the wrong person with your finances. The truth is that you should be able to trust financial professionals who hold themselves out as having expertise in managing money. Don't have the victim's mentality and blame yourself to the point that you fail to act. There are very respectable attorneys who can help you wade through these difficult circumstances. Given the specialized area, however, you should hire a lawyer with experience in securities arbitration.

Please check www.Sink-Swim.com for calculators, updates, and additional information, such as articles and links to valuable outside resources. Also, read the Sink or Swim blog and join in the discussion group.

Part IV

HOW MUCH WILL
YOU NEED?

Retirement is among investors' biggest concerns. Yet surprisingly, few investors have a comprehensive road map to get them where they want to go. The right strategy and asset allocation plan can certainly help. But the best possible strategy is only talk without the discipline to make it happen. Investors must make the deposits their plans require and stay the course during inevitable market downturns.

Retirement plans have two equally important components:

1. Building an adequate nest egg.
2. Making the nest egg last forever.

The focus of this lesson is on the former.

Too Much Is Never a Problem

A secure retirement takes lots of capital. With younger retirement and longer life expectancy, the average retiree will spend more years retired than were spent working. Most couples should plan for the survivor to reach at least the age of 95.

How big does that nest egg need to be? Most people find that they need at least 70% to 100% of their pre-retirement income to live comfortably. Few of today's retirees expect to stay home and watch TV all day. They are younger, healthier, and anticipate a longer life than any generation before. Most expect that, after parachuting out of the working world, they'll hit the ground running with the newfound freedom to travel, pursue hobbies, and participate in community activities. Many financial planners working with active retirees find that their clients spend more money during their 60s and 70s than they did during their working years. The pace of spending slows down a bit once they reach their 80s, but increasing health expenses soon raise their total income needs again.

Do-It-Yourself

www.Sink-Swim.com

Retirement Nest Egg Calculator: Do you know how much it takes to create a secure retirement? Use this calculator to help determine what size your retirement nest egg should be.

To figure out how much capital is needed at retirement, there is a rule of thumb that investors should plan on withdrawal rates of not more than 5% of their accumulated capital each year. This range allows for sustainable income as well as growth of income to hedge inflation, and growth of capital. For each dollar of income needed above Social Security and pension income, count on needing a nest egg of at least $20. For instance, if you will need $10,000 a year of income from your investments, you should start out with at least $200,000.

Beware Simplistic Software

A word of caution if you're using retirement planning software, such as that provided by some leading mutual fund companies: Such calculators don't distinguish between average return rates and the range of possible outcomes. For example, if you plug an average 10% rate of return into one of these tools, the software doesn't point out that the range of possible returns for that portfolio may fall between 6% and 14% three quarters of the time over a long period. You now have a 50% chance of falling short of your goal because, in context, "average" means that 50% of the time you do better than projected and 50% of the time you do worse. In other words, you can't count on an average outcome, and your results could possibly be far below average.

A more conservative rate-of-return assumption may make better sense. By saving somewhat more based on the lower range of possible outcomes, you can improve your chances of meeting your objective from 50% to 90%. Now you have minimized any chance that you won't reach your objective and even set yourself up for a possible positive surprise.

Better yet, combine conservative projections with a "Monte Carlo" analysis to simulate future returns and get a feel for the range and distributions of possible outcomes. Straight-line assumptions just don't occur in the real world, and Monte Carlo analysis might provide a better model of the range of future possibilities. Many top-end financial planning software programs include Monte Carlo simulations in their modeling.

Other assumptions your software is making might be overly optimistic. If expected returns are based on past index performance, they don't account for expenses, and they assume that every penny is invested every second. That's worth maybe 1% to 2% per year. If your software calculates arithmetic averages rather than compound returns, that's worth another 1.5%. Finally, these programs usually assume that the next 30 years will look just like the past 30 years. Who knows how much to discount that? Perhaps 2% is appropriate. So, you might want to give the final "expected" return a 4% haircut. We are still making a guess, but now it's one that is educated and conservative.

Keep It Real

Investors need to recognize that, because all models are very crude approximations of reality, it pays to err comfortably on the side of conservatism. Few investors lament having too much money when retirement rolls around. On the other hand, for those who are too optimistic in their planning, there's always that job at McDonald's. Would you like fries with that order?

Success in the accumulation phase is directly related to three variables: starting early, investing enough, and attaining reasonable rates of return. The math is pretty elementary. The relationship between time, amount invested, rate of return, and ultimate results are pretty well known. The dreary reality is that success requires discipline, and that retirement planning must be given a high priority early in one's career. After all, hope is not an action plan!

Forecasting Your Retirement Needs

Estimating your retirement needs might be impossible when you are very young. If you are far from retirement date, you may be better served to set an annual savings and investment goal. People closer to retirement might find that budgeting tools can help them to set goals.

The wild cards are long-term care and health costs. Medicare and Medicaid are going to suck the economy dry, so err on the side of caution.

Do-It-Yourself

www.Sink-Swim.com

Home Budget Analysis: Analyze your budget, see where your money goes, and find out where you can improve!

After you know your income needs, you can determine how much capital from all sources is necessary to generate it. Simply add up your entire income needs. Then subtract your Social Security benefit, your pension income, and any other regular incomes you expect, like rents or royalties. The balance is your income need from your retirement capital. Divide that need by the sustainable withdrawal rate expressed as a percent, and it will give you the capital you need. For example, suppose you need $20,000 a year and select a withdrawal rate of 5%. You will need ($20,000 / 0.05 = $400,000). At a 4% sustainable withdrawal rate, that number is $500,000. So, just what rate is sustainable?

Do-It-Yourself

www.Sink-Swim.com

Savings Goals: What will it take to reach your savings goal? This financial calculator helps you find out.

Lesson 29 ─────────────

Sustainable Withdrawal Rates

The *sustainable withdrawal rate* is the percentage of the portfolio retirees can safely withdraw each year from their capital without running the risk of drawing it down to zero during their lifetime. That number is far lower than most people would guess. That means that you need more capital than you would assume in order to finance an abundant retirement.

Old Assumptions Are Hazardous to Your Wealth

The traditional financial planning assumption about retirement income generation goes something like this: Investors make 10% on average; they withdraw 6% per year; each year, the account balance and income grow by an average of 4%; the investors die rich, and their children receive a windfall. This sounds wonderful in theory, but it's a bust in the real world.

The fatal problem with the traditional assumption is that it does not account for the variability of returns in the real world facing the retiree. The author knows from past experience that projecting average returns forward in a straight line is totally inappropriate. Average returns count for nothing if a client's retirement precedes a period like the Depression or 1973–1974. At such times, a retiree's nest egg stands a high chance of self-liquidating.

The real world is much more complicated and risky than an "average" return might indicate.

A Pioneering Study

Three business professors from Trinity University of Texas—Philip L. Cooley, Carl M. Hubbard, and Daniel T. Walz—broke new ground with their 1998 paper "Retirement Savings: Choosing a Withdrawal Rate That Is Sustainable."[1] They employed historical backtesting to demonstrate the relationship between withdrawal rates, time horizon, and asset allocation. The results reveal that portfolio failure rates are directly related to time horizon and withdrawal rates and are influenced by asset allocation.

Using the S&P 500 and bonds in various combinations over varying time periods commencing in 1926, the study tracked failure rates against withdrawal amounts. Even in the best possible case, where there were no taxes, no expenses, no transaction fees, and the optimum portfolio was known in advance, significant failure rates occurred above 6% withdrawal rates (see Figure 29.1).

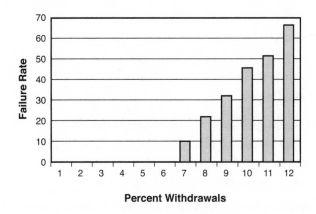

Percent Withdrawals

Figure 29.1   Failure rate with optimum portfolios: 30-year periods

[1] *American Association of Individual Investors Journal,* 20(2): 16–21.

The Cooley, Hubbard, and Walz study highlights the need for conservative withdrawal rates and, by implication, the need to accumulate liberal amounts of capital to fund a comfortable retirement. Historical back-testing is a useful tool and provides a powerful "sanity check." However, like any modeling tool, it has limitations. In this case, our example sticks us with only one series of data. Unless you believe that the past results will reoccur in exactly the same sequence, our findings will not be as robust as you might hope. For instance, running the sequence backward or any other re-shuffling will result in entirely different results. Furthermore, historical back-testing leaves us with no simple method to vary either rates of return or volatility in the sample set.

New and more powerful modeling tools confirm these principles and add additional insight, but do not replace the need for very conservative assumptions if the retiree wishes to have a high probability of success.

The fact remains that the highest risk factor you, as a retiree, face, and the only decision directly under your control, is the withdrawal rate.

Summary

It's hard to overestimate the importance of selecting a realistic withdrawal rate.

- Withdrawals impose a heavy risk on the portfolio.
- Even if you expect an average 10% return on your portfolio, you can't withdraw anything close to that because of the risk of sucking the portfolio dry in down markets.
- If capital is insufficient, the retiree might be tempted to increase the withdrawal rate.

- A high withdrawal rate increases the chance of going broke.
- Reaching for higher investment returns increases volatility, which in turn increases the chance of going broke.

As a rule of thumb, you should be very comfortable with a 4% rate of withdrawal, reasonably comfortable with a 5% rate, uncomfortable with a 6% rate, and scared out of your mind with any rate higher than that.

Lesson 30 ————————————

Forecasting Your Needs

Forecasting your exact retirement needs may be impossible, but that doesn't mean you shouldn't plan for the lifestyle you want.

Early in Your Career

Nobody can make an accurate financial forecast over a 40-year time horizon. A tiny little change in assumptions will grow to an enormous change in outcomes. It's delusional to think anything else.

But, if you are early in your career, don't throw up your hands and do nothing. If you can't set a realistic retirement income goal today, you can still plan for your retirement. Set a savings goal, invest wisely, and keep the discipline over your entire career.

Even relatively modest amounts grow to significant retirement capital over a long time horizon. But, it's important that you keep the money in play over that long horizon.

For instance, starting at age 22, $500 a month ($6,000 a year) saved for 10 years at 8% net return grows to $86,919. But, even if you make no further contributions, the value of that account grows because of compounding to $874,636 by the time you are 62 and $1,101,789 at age 65.

Do-It-Yourself

www.Sink-Swim.com

Compound Interest and Your Return: This calculator demonstrates how compounding can affect your savings.

Cool Million: Find out when your savings plan might make you a millionaire!

Don't Delay Your Savings! Waiting to begin your savings plan can have a huge impact on your results. This calculator helps show you how much postponing your savings plan can really cost.

Savings Calculator: Find out how consistent investments over a number of years can be an effective strategy to accumulate wealth.

As your income goes up, you ought to increase your savings. But, even if you keep saving the same amount, it grows to $1,554,339, a worthy sum over 40 years. In just three more years, it grows to $1,977,498. So, when you are ready to retire, something meaningful will be there. If you choose a 4% withdrawal rate from your nest egg, you can provide yourself with $62,173 of income for the rest of your life at age 62, or $79,899 at 65.

This simple example holds several important lessons for us. We will be coming back to it.

You might be whining that you can't afford a $500-a-month savings objective. However, that's the amount of a monthly, entry-level, luxury car payment. Which would you rather have: a five-series BMW today, or about $60,000 to $80,000 a year in retirement? It is up to you.

As a rule of thumb, you should aim to put a total of 15% of your pre-tax income into a retirement plan and savings. Of course, you need to invest it efficiently and effectively.

Later in Your Career

Late in your career, a budget may be a useful tool to plan your post-retirement expenses. But you are still going to have to make some interesting choices about lifestyle and values. Do you really want to "downsize" your lifestyle, or move to Costa Rica? Can you give up the golf club membership or, alternatively, will you find a life of endless golf boring beyond belief?

The closer you are to retirement, and the less you expect to change your lifestyle, the easier it is to make a realistic budget. And although your budget probably won't capture everything about your new life expenses, at least it's a place to start. You may be thinking that you would rather have a root canal than do a budget. Well, just suck it up and do it. You can't plan anything without knowing how much you need to spend. When you are done, reward yourself with your favorite candy bar or a nice glass of wine. You can find a basic budget online at www.Sink-Swim.com.

---

www.Sink-Swim.com

Do-It-Yourself

Home Budget Analysis: Analyze your budget, see where your money goes, and find out where you can improve!

If you are planning radical changes, you might need to do some research. Just what is the cost of your Starbucks latte on the French Riviera? How much will it cost to import your car into Honduras? What's the quality of the local medical community, and does your insurance pay for treatment, in Thailand? After taxes and transaction costs, will it really save you anything to move to that retirement home in Arizona? After all, what you save in heating oil may very well be spent on air conditioning.

Most of us experience our highest earnings late in our career. We all also find ways to increase our spending to accommodate our new earning levels. Most of us have a "lifestyle" inflation as we go through our careers. We seamlessly graduate to bigger houses, newer and more expensive cars, a taste for better wine, foreign travel, and nicer restaurants. We spoil our grandchildren and indulge our spouses.

Having tasted these delectable delights, we are understandably reluctant to give them up. As a baseline for retirement planning, we probably want to continue with most of our new indulgences. That means we need a high percentage of our immediate pre-retirement income.

The Three-Phase Model of Retirement: Is It Valid for You?

Your income needs will be different in retirement, but they might not be constant across the years. Using other people's experiences may not be particularly helpful to you. But, they might give you a clue as you try to puzzle out your own situation.

Many financial planners divide retirement into three phases. The common perception that expenses decline after retirement might not hold true for you. Some retirees find that initially they need more than their pre-retirement income as they satisfy some delayed gratification demands. Those could conceivably include travel, a new boat, hobbies, or a second home.

After a few years of shamelessly indulging themselves, retirees might tend to slow down to smell the roses. At this point, living expenses may fall.

Finally, late in life, retirees often find that medical expenses and assisted living arrangements require additional income and resources that push their expenditures far above their pre-retirement income.

The three-phase model may not be particularly accurate. At best, it's a gross oversimplification because it is difficult to identify what may be described as a "typical" retiree. People find their own path without following anybody else's script. Life unfolds differently than you plan. It's hard to imagine how you will want to spend your days 20 years from now.

Of course, the one wild card in the whole pack is the inability to forecast your future health. Life and financial requirements look entirely different after a disability or general decline in health. Even if you stay healthy and active, insurance costs are almost impossible to predict. Medicare and Medicaid are even bigger financial black holes than Social Security, so how much help you might get from the various federal government programs is problematic. Count on picking up an increasing part of the load yourself.

It looks like having too much capital at retirement is not going to be a major problem for most retirees as they survey their future funding needs. But, any plan you devise must be flexible enough to satisfy your varying requirements as you age.

Gap Analysis

After you have done a reasonable budget, take a look at your sources of income to see how the two compare.

Sources of income might include Social Security, defined benefit pension plans, military or government retirement plans, rents, or royalties. If you are fortunate enough to have income from a trust account, include that, too.

Any shortfall or gap needs to be made up from your investment accounts, both tax-deferred and taxable. Those investment accounts would include IRAs, Roth IRAs, 401(k), 403(b), and 457 accounts, as well as your private brokerage accounts.

If you expect to receive an inheritance, it might be prudent to exclude that from your calculations until the estate is settled. You wouldn't be the first boomer to find that your parents joyfully spent your inheritance.

Accounting for Outside Incomes in Asset Allocation

The question is often asked about how to account for fixed income during retirement. For instance, Betty, a retiree, has a military pension of $20,000, Social Security of $15,000, rental income of $10,000, and a fixed annuity of $5,000 for life. She also owns an IRA rollover account worth $1 million and a brokerage account worth $500,000. She has done her budget, and believes that she needs an annual income of $100,000 pre-tax and adjusted for inflation to meet her retirement needs.

In cases like this, the first question might be how to adjust the asset allocation plan to account for the fixed income streams. Can she offset and reduce the bond requirement by the amount of the fixed income?

That is not necessary, or even a good idea. Betty has a certain gross income need. She has certain fixed or outside income cash flows. The fixed income, Social Security, pension, rental income, and annuity payments are out of our control as investment managers. These fixed incomes offset the total income need, but probably shouldn't be included in the investment account asset allocation.

As always, there might be exceptions. For instance, if you own a large amount of rental real estate, you might not want more real estate exposure in your retirement portfolio. And if you have a couple of oil wells in your back yard, then commodities futures might not offer a meaningful diversification benefit for your unique financial situation.

What you want to focus on is how much income must the investment accounts generate to make up the gap between the outside known fixed income and the desired retirement income?

Betty has a certain amount of capital (in this case, $1.5 million from the combined IRA and brokerage accounts), and she needs to generate a certain amount of income from it each year to meet her retirement needs (in this case, $50,000, the difference between the $100,000 and the sum of the fixed payments of $50,000 from the four outside sources).

The military pension and Social Security will probably be adjusted for inflation. The rental income may be, and the annuity payment will probably not be. Therefore, she needs to adjust each yearly income requirement for inflation. A good spreadsheet handles that in seconds.

As a result, Betty needs to generate $50,000 a year reliably from an investment pool of $1.5 million. That's a very conservative withdrawal rate from the available capital, and if responsibly invested, should have a high probability of lasting forever while providing growth of capital and income. The asset allocation recommendation will be identical to the case where there was no outside income, but the investor had the same amount of investable capital and income need.

By focusing in on the investment capital available and the income that it needs to generate, she avoids the distraction of how to capitalize the outside income flows, and how to adjust the asset allocation to account for it. Suddenly, the appropriate asset allocation to accomplish her goals becomes a lot clearer. The method simplifies the problem and gets better answers at the same time.

How Are You Doing?

Are you on track for a successful retirement? Check out the calculator at www.Sink-Swim.com.

---

www.Sink-Swim.com

Do-It-Yourself

Retirement Planner: Quickly determine if your retirement plan is on track—and learn how to keep it there.

Retirement Shortfall: Running out of your retirement savings too soon is one of the biggest risks to a comfortable retirement. Use this calculator to find a potential shortfall in your current retirement savings plan.

Please check www.Sink-Swim.com for calculators, updates, and additional information, such as articles and links to valuable outside resources. Also, read the Sink or Swim blog and join in the discussion group.

Part V

INVESTING TO MEET YOUR GOALS

Lesson 31

The Anti-Cramer Guide to Investment Success

You can invest effectively and economically. Investing is a lot simpler than many people think. But today's media is not going to be much help. There are no fewer than three cable TV networks devoted exclusively to covering the market. Listening to them will fill your head with garbage.

Jim Cramer's TV world, for instance, revolves around active management: market forecasts and individual stock and bond selection. In short, he worships at the temple of the inefficient market. Cramer's show is amusing and entertaining, but you mustn't take it seriously. There is no credible evidence anywhere that active management can consistently add value to the investment process. In fact, the overwhelming weight of the evidence shows that it reduces returns while adding risk. Although he has captured lots of popular attention, his world view is diametrically opposed to everything we have learned about finance in the last 50 years

Modern financial theory is an alternative world view that, if applied consistently, is much more likely to lead to a successful investment experience.

You can construct an effective portfolio that is low cost, low risk (relatively), tax efficient, and matched to your individual need for liquidity and risk tolerance.

Lesson 32

Start Early

The earlier you start, the easier the task of securing your comfortable retirement. The magic of continuously compounding returns makes the goal easily achievable.

So, you are thinking about retirement. Someday you ought to start a savings and investment plan so that you can retire, or at least have the option to retire. But, you want a new car, need this season's wardrobe with those neat new colors, and last year's vacation bills are still on the credit card. You decide to put it off for a while.

This makes you just like most other Americans who collectively have close to a zero after-tax savings rate. So, it's not exactly like anybody else will notice. If asked, you might answer that your most important financial concern is having enough for a comfortable retirement. Nevertheless, you prefer to think about it tomorrow.

Economists have long been puzzled by the contradiction. You want to retire someday, yet you are not saving for it. They have a great technical explanation: You discount distant events at a different rate than nearer ones. People often mistakenly believe that what they are doing today is far more important than what they will be doing years from now. What this means is that you want the new car *now*!

Who Wants to Be a Millionaire?

Who could be a millionaire? Almost everybody. It makes you wonder why there aren't more. Perhaps most folks would only like to be a millionaire if someone would just give them the money. They don't want it bad enough to plan or—oh, no!—save.

But, wait! Did I say that almost everybody could be a millionaire? You heard me right.

Let's say that you just left college at age 22. You put $3,574 away each year and net 8%. By the time you are 62, you have your million. That's less than $300 a month (see Table 32.1). Of course, if you got 11%, you would only have to put away $1,719, or less than $150 per month. But, 11% net is outside the bounds of likely outcomes. Don't bet the farm on the very best possible case scenario.

Perhaps, though, you should consider the enormous cost of waiting to begin to fund your retirement. Every day you delay means a higher annual cost to meet the same goal, and that you will have to contribute far more in total than if you started earlier.

Table 32.1   Deposits Required to Reach $1,000,000 at 8%

Years to Retirement	40	30	20	15	10	5	1
Monthly Deposit	$297.83	$681.17	$1,686.17	$2,841.75	$5,623.33	$13,152.50	$77,160.50
Annual Deposit	$3,574.00	$8,174.00	$20,234.00	$34,101.00	$63,916.00	$157,830.00	$925,926.00
Total Deposit	$142,969.00	$245,206.00	$404,671.00	$511,521.00	$639,162.00	$789,150.00	$925,926.00

In Figure 32.1, notice how much your annual deposits required increase as time decreases.

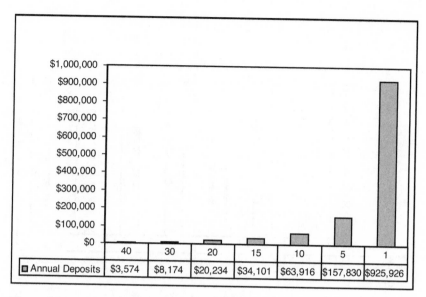

	40	30	20	15	10	5	1
▫ Annual Deposits	$3,574	$8,174	$20,234	$34,101	$63,916	$157,830	$925,926

Figure 32.1   Annual deposits to meet goal

Because your deposits are earning and compounding over time, growth of the account contributes a major part of the total goal. The longer you wait to start, the less it can contribute. So, your out-of-pocket cost goes up with delay (see Figure 32.2).

---

www.Sink-Swim.com

Do-It-Yourself

Cool Million: Find out when your savings plan may make you a millionaire!

Savings Calculator: Find out how consistent investments over a number of years can be an effective strategy to accumulate wealth.

Savings Goals: What will it take to reach your savings goal? This financial calculator helps you find out.

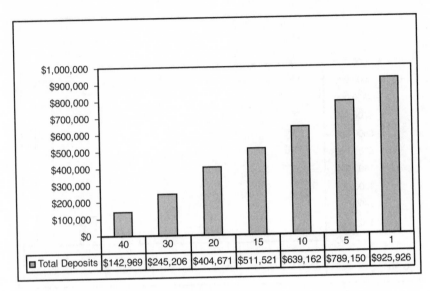

| Total Deposits | $142,969 | $245,206 | $404,671 | $511,521 | $639,162 | $789,150 | $925,926 |

Figure 32.2   Total deposits required

For instance, if you have 40 years to go until retirement, your total out-of-pocket cost to meet your million-dollar goal is $142,969. That's only about $300 a month. The rest came from growth. But, if you wait for ten years, your total out-of-pocket cost grows to $245,206. The additional $102,237 over your remaining 30 years is the cost of delay!

The simple moral to this story is start early and keep time on your side. Every second of delay increases your cost and makes it harder to meet your goal. Today would be a really good day to start saving!

Get Market Rates of Return

Most people don't come close to getting the earning rates they should over their lifetimes. Invest in equities through thick and thin. Keep a long-term horizon and ignore the short-term noise.

Failure to obtain a market rate of return raises your costs dramatically. Reaching the same goal requires substantially more savings if your portfolio returns just 8% rather than 10%.

How much would you need to invest per year to get to $1,000,000? Refer to Table 32.2.

Table 32.2   Deposits Required to Reach $1,000,000 at Different Returns

	30 Years	20 Years	15 Years	10 Years	5 Years
At 8% Annual Return	$8,173	$20,233	$34,101	$63,916	$157,830
At 10% Annual Return	$5,526	$15,872	$28,612	$57,041	$148,906

Do-It-Yourself

www.Sink-Swim.com

Compound Interest and Your Return: This calculator demonstrates how compounding can affect your savings.

Compare Savings Rates: Even a small difference in the interest you are paid on your savings can add up over time. Use this calculator to see how different savings rates can impact your savings strategy!

What Are Reasonable Expectations for Market Returns?

If you are assuming a return higher than the long-term historical averages, you are kidding yourself. If your plan is built on an assumption over 10% net, you probably will fail. You can't directly control the ultimate investment rate, but you can control how much you save.

The entire U.S. stock market returned 10.15% annualized from January 1926 to December 2006. That's before any taxes, expenses, or other friction. As a planning tool, you might want to use a net rate of 8% or 9%. No one knows what it really will be, but that's within the range of reasonableness. Of course, that's only equities. If you have a bond portion in your portfolio, the estimate should be reduced accordingly. There is no point in fooling yourself with a high rate of return assumption. Never do your planning as if the very best possible scenario is the likely outcome.

Manage Risk, Don't Avoid It

Paradoxically, not taking enough investment risk may guarantee failure. Risk decreases over time. Strange as it may seem, over longer periods, the risky asset is the high-probability shot. Therefore, the worst-case estimate for stocks is almost better than the best-case estimate for bonds.

Bonds and other savings alternatives do not offer enough real total return to meet reasonable economic needs later. Early in your career, a 100% global equity portfolio properly diversified with some low-cost index funds and ETFs has the highest chance of a successful outcome over long time periods. Later, you must scale back the risk as your retirement date approaches.

Lesson 33 —————————————

Cleaning Up Credit Card Debt

Many people use credit cards responsibly. They buy no more than they can afford and pay off the entire balance each month. Properly used, they are a major convenience. Who in their right mind wants to haul around piles of cash just to buy milk at the grocery store?

Then there are credit card junkies. They finance their lifestyle on easy credit while sinking any chance to develop a net worth. Their debt and service costs just grow and grow as they indulge themselves while making or occasionally missing the minimum monthly payment schedule. You know which one you are.

Giving up your credit card habit may be tougher than quitting smoking, but it's just as important to your financial health as cleaning up your lungs is to your physical well-being.

It is easy to think that you should start to save and invest while carrying a credit card debt. But, credit card debt (and other consumer debt) is ugly through and through. You can't swim or even tread water carrying that kind of load. You have a better chance of swimming a mile while carrying 20 lbs. of lead weights. Your first step toward financial independence is to eliminate all consumer debt and keep free of it. Your goal is to zero out the balance each month. Failing that, cut the cards up into little tiny pieces, pay them off, and don't use them again. Use debit cards instead for your cash and purchase needs.

Total credit card costs include a confusing variety of fees and interest at rates that vary at the whim of the card company. Few cardholders understand the total impact of these charges against their outstanding balances. A cynical person might think that the disclosures credit card companies must provide are deliberately misleading, confusing, opaque, and evasive. But, the total charges can vary from 18 to more than 36 percent. That's significantly higher than any reasonable investment return you could assume.

Let's consider the case of a couple with $10,000 in long-term investments and a $10,000 credit card debt. So, looking at just those two accounts, they have a net worth of zero.

If you put a gun to my head, the most liberal guesstimate I could make on the long-term prospects of an equity investment account would be 11%. But, there is a good argument that going forward, returns might be closer to 8%. So, under our most optimistic assumption, that account might earn $1,100 in an average year. But, the credit card debt is costing somewhere between $1,800 and $3,600+. Our net worth is going backward!

By now, you should have rightly observed that liquidating the savings account to pay off the credit card debt is the rational way to go. By extension, then, paying off any outstanding credit card debt should be a priority before beginning an investment program.

If you can't pay off the credit card debt today, but you haven't already totally destroyed your credit rating, you may be able to transfer it to a credit card offering short-term "teaser" rates. Like a good drug pusher, they are anxious to get you hooked on their stuff, so they are offering "free" or almost free introductory rates. This might give you a chance to play them off against each other while you dig yourself out of debt.

Do-It-Yourself

www.Sink-Swim.com

Cost-of-Debt Calculator: Use this calculator to see just how expensive paying interest on your debt can be.

Credit Card Minimum Payment Calculator: Use this calculator to determine how long it will take you to pay off your credit cards if you only make the minimum payments.

Credit Card Optimizer: The Credit Card Optimizer helps you determine the best distribution of your credit card debt.

Credit Card Pay Off: Use this calculator to see what it will take to pay off your credit card balance, and what you can change to meet your repayment goals.

Pay off the highest-cost cards first, and roll that debt down to lower-cost cards as possible. Keep at it until you are debt-free.

Do-It-Yourself

www.Sink-Swim.com

Roll-Down Your Credit Card Debt! The Credit Card Roll-Down Calculator applies two simple principles to paying off your credit card debt.

If you are in over your head, you may be able to negotiate with the card companies for some relief. Somewhere, there may be a legitimate credit counseling service, but so many of them are outright scams that it's hard to recommend that approach. Far too many folks end up with no relief and another pile of bills after succumbing to the lure of credit repair schemes. When you see those ads on TV, loud little bells and bright flashing lights ought to be going off inside your head. Don't go there.

Do-It-Yourself

Personal Debt Consolidation: Should you consolidate your debt? This calculator is designed to help determine if debt consolidation is right for you.

As a last resort, you might consider a second mortgage. But, don't go down that road unless it's the last time you do. Systematically destroying your home equity to feed your credit card addiction is a road to ruin.

Refinancing gives you an opportunity to make the situation even worse by accepting one of the sub-prime mortgage products with teaser rates, variable interest charges sure to escalate, and 100% equity-to-debt ratios. Those toxic financial products have devastated thousands of families. It might appear to be a lifeline but, more likely, it's a mine that can blow up on contact. If you must re-finance, stick to traditional fixed-rate mortgage products.

After you have cleaned up your credit card debts, you can begin to build a financial future of saving and investment on a sound foundation.

Lesson 34

Costs Matter

Returns in the world's equity markets are liberal, but finite. Anything you spend on fund management fees reduces those returns.

Mutual funds have two kinds of expenses: fully disclosed, and those that must be imputed. Disclosed expenses include management fees and loads.

- Management fees include paying the managers, research, and expenses for accounting, legal, customer support, compliance, and sending reports to investors. Lower costs are better.

- Sales loads or charges include front-end commissions (A shares), back-end or contingent sales charges (B shares), level loads (C shares), and 12(b)-1 fees. None of these add value to the investor. Avoid them all. Just say no. There is an entire world of no-load, low-cost index funds that provide exposure to every market in the world. Never pay a sales load. Deal directly with a fund family like Vanguard, or purchase through a discount brokerage like Schwab, TD Ameritrade, or Fidelity for a nominal transaction fee.

---

www.Sink-Swim.com

Do-It-Yourself

Mutual Fund Expense Calculator: This calculator can help you analyze the costs associated with buying shares in a mutual fund. By entering a few pieces of information, found in your fund's prospectus, you can see the impact of fees and operating expenses on your investment.

The cost of trading within a fund is not disclosed. It includes commissions the fund must pay, and market impact. Where turnover in a portfolio is great, these costs are often as much or more than the disclosed costs. Stick with funds with low turnover. Index funds have only trivial turnover compared to their actively managed competitors.

Simply moving from managed mutual funds to index funds may save you as much as 1.5% to 2.00% a year. That's huge over the life of your portfolio. For instance: Invest $1,000 a year for 30 years at 8%, and the total accumulation is $113,283.21. But, at 7%, it's only $94,460.78. That's a difference of $18,822.42.

Mutual fund expenses, or brokerage fees and commissions, can eat up over 1.5% of your market returns if you are not careful. Use no-load index funds.

Controlling Investment Costs: Churning and Twisting

The bottom line is that investment costs cut into your returns, especially over the long term. Over time, they can have a negative impact on your retirement savings. From a legal perspective, brokerage firms can be held liable for charging their clients excessive commissions or fees. From a practical standpoint, however, the high costs paid for investments may not be substantial enough to warrant filing an individual lawsuit, and the brokerage firms and insurance companies know it. Therefore, you really need to be aware of how much you are paying for investment products and commissions. When it comes to fees, most of the time it is really swim at your own risk!

A common area of abuse involves charging excessive commissions—churning. *Churning* occurs when a broker buys and sells investments, such as stocks in your account, in order to generate excessive commissions. Churning is a breach of a broker's duty to recommend suitable investments and investment strategies. The incidents of churning in brokerage accounts appear to have decreased in recent years because brokerage firms' compliance departments have gotten better at catching brokers who do this. I have represented many churning victims, and the clients typically have good cases.

As always, the best way to avoid becoming a victim is to educate yourself about how brokerage firms charge you for their services and to know in advance what type of investor you are. In general, brokerage firms have two types of accounts: commission-based accounts and fee-based accounts. Commission-based accounts charge a commission per trade, while fee-based accounts charge clients a percent of the assets in the account (typically 1%–2%), regardless of the number of trades made. To know which is cheaper, you need to know whether you are an active trader (that is, someone who intends to buy and sell investments frequently) or a "buy and hold" investor (that is, someone who intends to buy an investment and hold it for a long time). After you know this, you can compare prices.

You might be saying to yourself, "I don't know what type of investor I am. That is what I pay my broker to know." If you fall into this category, you are asking for trouble. At a minimum, however, ask your brokers how they intend to manage your money. Do they plan to trade your account actively, or do they intend to buy a few investments upfront and hold them for the long term? How do they get paid: commissions, fees, or a combination of both? How much, how often? Demand full disclosure of all relevant costs.

In the annuity context, the term "twisting" is used, but it is really the same thing as churning. *Twisting* involves buying and selling annuities for the purpose of generating commissions. Typically, the broker tells you that your existing annuity is inadequate and that you need a better one. The broker often tells the client that the new product has an upfront bonus, which offsets any surrender charges on the existing annuity, and that there are no tax consequences. Don't buy it! The new annuity will have a whole new surrender charge penalty period and will often be more expensive than your previous annuity. On many of these new products, especially the misleadingly named Equity-Linked Index Annuities, the broker gets paid very high commissions (more than 10%) upfront. The insurance company makes up for the high commissions by locking up your money for years and charging you an arm and a leg. The best way to avoid becoming a victim of twisting is not to buy an annuity in the first place!

—*Contributed by Jason Doss*

Lesson 35

Taxes Matter

Taxes are the biggest cost investors face. They are a dead drag on performance. Every cent that marches off the field to the IRS is not there for you to use for retirement. It's never coming back! Obviously, it's only prudent to manage taxes.

But, remember, minimizing taxes is not the objective; maximizing after-tax returns is the objective. Turnover in an investment portfolio is the worst offender in generating taxes. Each time a stock is sold, the taxable gain is distributed to the shareholders. With some actively managed funds turning over more than 200%, any gains would be taxed at the highest marginal tax rate of the holder.

Index funds are low-turnover by comparison, and therefore naturally tax-efficient. Even more tax-sensitive index funds have evolved that have adopted accounting rules and reduced turnover to manage the tax drag further.

Maximize use of tax-favored vehicles like IRAs and pension plans. Use tax-efficient funds with low turnover in your personal accounts. Buy and hold.

www.Sink-Swim.com

Do-It-Yourself

Compare Investment Fees: You will find that even a small difference in the fees you pay on your investments can add up over time. Use this calculator to see how different fees impact your investment strategy!

Investment Returns: Use this calculator to help you see how inflation, taxes, and your time horizon can impact your bottom line. There is more to investing than knowing your annual rate of return.

Municipal Bond Tax Equivalent Yield: Should you be using municipal bonds? Income generated from municipal bond coupon payments are not subject to federal income tax and often are exempt from state taxes. Use this calculator to estimate the tax-equivalent yield (TEY) for a municipal bond.

Lesson 36

Control Risk

A properly diversified portfolio has a much higher probability of success than does a risky one. Aim for the lowest risk possible that will meet your investment rate of return goal.

Risk and Reward Are Related

Investors are systematically rewarded for accepting risk. You cannot expect to have real returns in the markets unless you accept some risk. Treasury bills, CDs, and money market funds have historically generated almost exactly the rate of inflation. On an after-tax basis, they are losers.

Investment advisors and economists are fond of using the term "standard deviation" to measure risk. This term is useless in conversation with the average investor. However, if you were to substitute this with the term "relative risk rating," investors would most likely get it. Higher standard deviations (relative risk ratings) are riskier in that they fluctuate through a greater range during their life.

Because investors hate risk and prefer certain outcomes, in order to tempt them away from their treasury bills and CDs, risky assets must offer the prospect of higher returns. The market does this by pricing risky assets lower relative to their expected earnings than safe ones. Because they are a lower-priced relative to their expected earnings, risky assets have higher expected returns. Markets fine-tune these relationships on almost an instantaneous basis through price adjustments of securities.

This relationship is so well-documented that it's almost a physical law. You can plot asset class returns on a graph against risk and find that they all fall very close to the line that connects the zero-risk asset with the market as a whole. Economists call this the Capital Market Line (CML). You may safely forget the term once you understand that risk and reward are related.

There are no high-return, low-risk assets. Markets are far too efficient to allow that to happen. If you think you have one, you are delusional. You might as well expect to fall upward. If someone attempts to sell you one, that person is either a liar or incompetent.

Controlling Risk

Investors focus with a laser-like intensity on a single factor of investment success: rate of return. Why? Because rate of return is simple to understand, and focusing on it reduces the entire multidimensional problem to a single number. A good strategy, or a good investment manager, has a high rate of return. A bad strategy or investment manager has a low rate of return. If only life were that simple!

By focusing on rate of return and ignoring risk, investors may torpedo themselves. High-risk strategies, even those that have high returns, may decrease the chance of an investor having a successful experience. Within a wide band, investors may be far better served to focus on managing risk than stretching for additional return.

Few investors have an intuitive feel for the impact of risk. Just mention standard deviation, and most of them will zone right out. It would be helpful if advisors replaced the term "standard deviation" with "relative risk rating." In addition, fund managers should be required to place equal emphasis on risk rating along with rate of return and publish relevant comparative data for the appropriate indexes.

Managing risk isn't nearly as glamorous as generating excess returns. But, excess returns are elusive, while basic risk management is easily achieved.

Diversification reduces risk without compromising rate of return. An investor choosing between two strategies with equal expected returns would certainly prefer the one with a lower risk. Lower risk not only reduces the dispersion of returns; it also increases both median and average returns. High-risk strategies may produce a few winners with outsized returns, but many more investors will experience substandard and unsatisfactory results. Investors are concerned with the certainty of results. After all, if you are dead broke, it's a small consolation that somewhere else is an investor who struck it rich.

An Accumulation Example

Table 36.1 shows the distribution of returns for different theoretical risk levels. Let's assume a 10% average return, a $100,000 beginning balance, a 30-year timeframe, and standard deviations of 10%, 20%, and 30%, respectively. Feeding these assumptions into a Monte Carlo simulator shows how important managing risk is.

Table 36.1   Risk Matters: Higher Risk Leads to Lower Median Returns

Standard Deviation	Average Return	Best Case	Worst Case	Median
10%	$1,730,329	$7,569,806	$186,925	$1,534,396
20%	$1,699,584	$25,313,829	$16,146	$1,060,438
30%	$1,641,217	$65,208,720	$1,171	$585,919

As you can see, as risk levels increase while holding rate of return constant, results become skewed. The average returns are virtually identical. But, both the best results and worst become more extreme. A few trials yield mega results, balancing out the trials that fall under the average. Importantly, the median result decreases precipitously as risk increases. More and more trials fall below the average result. This lower median return is the "cost" of the higher risk strategy.

The finding is consistent with the widely understood concept of variance drag. Because of variance drag, average (arithmetic) returns are always above compound (geometric) returns by an amount that increases as the volatility of the portfolio increases. Only when there is no volatility are they the same. Volatility reduces the returns that investors care about—the compound return that ends up in their pockets.

Because there are no withdrawals in the preceding illustrations, none of the portfolios crash and burn. But, when we introduce systematic withdrawals, the probability of portfolio failure increases with the withdrawal rate. During down markets, so much capital to fund disbursements is consumed at depressed prices to fund disbursements that the portfolio may self-liquidate. So, it's essential that wherever there are systematic withdrawals from a portfolio, risk should be vigorously controlled. Higher risk leads to predictably higher portfolio failures. Retirees, charitable institutions, endowment funds, and defined benefit pension plans must exercise prudence when managing their funds or risk portfolio blow out.

Risk Is Amplified with Systematic Withdrawals

Table 36.2 shows the results at various risk levels for a portfolio taking systematic withdrawals. Assume that you have $100,000 beginning capital, a $6,000 dollar-a-year withdrawal beginning year one, a 30-year time horizon, and 10%, 20%, and 30% standard deviation. A successful portfolio is considered one with $1 remaining after 30 years.

Table 36.2   Risk Matters: As Risk Increases During Withdrawals, Portfolio Failures Increase

Standard Deviation	Average Remaining Capital	Best Case	Worst Case	Median Remaining Capital	Probability of Failure
10%	$749,508	$ 4,801,855	$0	$615,244	1%
20%	$759,208	$18,387,065	$0	$318,072	21%
30%	$782,699	$50,637,405	$0	$52,577	43%

See Sink-Swim.com for real case post-mortem.

Summary

Diversification is the cardinal rule of investment management. Diversification reduces risk and increases the probability of a successful outcome for the investor. Concentrated stock positions violate every principle of modern portfolio practice standards. They are neither suitable nor prudent for the vast majority of investors.

Prudent diversification reduces risk without sacrificing expected rates of return. Global diversification is the gold standard for prudence in equities. A portfolio must be tailored to the liquidity needs, risk preferences, and time horizon of the client. Short-term, high-quality bonds provide a store of value without significant market risk to meet those liquidity needs.

Over a reasonable range, reducing risk is more important than chasing incremental returns. The appropriate portfolio is the one that offers the highest probability of success rather than the highest return regardless of the risk level. In many cases, investors may even increase their chance of a successful outcome by opting for a portfolio with lower returns and risk.

Determine Your Risk Tolerance and Time Horizon

It goes without saying that you should take no more risk than you find comfortable, and no more risk than is necessary to reach your objectives.

Risk avoidance is not an option for most investors. You can certainly build a zero-risk portfolio, but it is not likely to get you where you need to be. For example, suppose you wanted 100% of your current income (inflation adjusted) when you retire in 30 years. The income would continue for an additional 30 years, and then the principal would be exhausted. However, you are not willing to take any risk in your investment portfolio. You could simply invest in treasury bills, the U.S. zero-risk asset. Treasury bills are not subject to default because the government can always print more dollars, and the market prices them continuously at just about the inflation rate. Here is the problem: Because the real rate of return is effectively zero, you need to invest 50% of your gross income to meet this goal. Given that most of us pay taxes, a 50% savings rate is not feasible.

The unpleasant reality that zero-risk investments are zero-real-growth means that you must accept some level of risk to obtain reasonable economic goals with your savings and investments. Assuming too little risk may absolutely guarantee that the investor will fail to meet his goals.

Rather than attempt to avoid risk, your task is to manage a comfortable level of risk to obtain an optimum return. How much risk should you take? First, the investor must understand both his time horizon and risk tolerance. Both are important.

Time horizon is the time until the portfolio, or a portion of it, is liquidated for some other use. If you need money to purchase a boat next year, that's a definite time horizon. If the money is to come out of your investment account, you need to account for it. But, if it is to come from current income, you can ignore it in our portfolio construction.

However, if you want to retire next year and expect to require income from your investments, your time investment horizon is the rest of your life. But, each annual income need for the next several years needs to be considered. It couldn't be much simpler. Just add up all the projected cash outflows from the account for the next 5 to 10 years and keep that much in very stable, safe assets.

In very general terms, no funds that need to be withdrawn from the portfolio in the near- to mid-term ought to be invested at risk in the equity market. Otherwise, you run the risk of having to liquidate stocks in a down market to fund a cash flow that was known in advance. That's not what investing is all about.

The balance might be invested in risky assets for the long-term growth you need to meet your objectives. If that division of assets between risk-free and risky assets is too risky to allow you a good night's sleep, then you need to reduce the equity holdings further until you can sleep soundly as the market goes through its normal gyrations.

It's important that investors determine their risk tolerance in advance and stick to it. There is nothing quite so destructive to long-term investing as bailing out during normal market declines, only to repurchase at a higher cost after the market has righted itself. Far too many investors buy high, sell low, endlessly repeat the process, and then wonder why they don't make money in the capital markets.

How can you determine how much risk to take and build a portfolio that meets your unique needs? Read on.

Risk management is more important than trying to increase returns. It's easy to manage risk: Diversify prudently. It's hard to impossible to beat the market, and you can destroy your portfolio in the attempt.

Lesson 37————————————————

Concentrated Stock

Concentrating investments into one single company, just a few stocks, a sector such as tech stocks or financials, or a single country exposes the investor to enormous risk that is not going to be compensated. All these risks must be diversified away. The higher the concentration in a portfolio, the higher the risk that something awful might happen. Don't do it. Diversification is the ultimate investor protection. Use it to prosper and sleep well at night.

Don't Put All Your Eggs in One Basket

Everyone has heard this cliché, but it couldn't be more true in the world of investments. Many clients' entire nest eggs get decimated because the broker gambles on the future of a particular stock or sector of stocks (for example, technology stocks in 2000).

Your broker has the duty to recommend that your account be diversified among such different investment classes as cash, stocks, and bonds, and across wide industry sectors (such as technology, energy, industrials, consumer staples, healthcare, and banking/financial) within classes. A properly diversified account is the best possible way to minimize your risk and avoid excessive losses.

Over-concentration occurs when the investments in your portfolio are disproportionately weighted in one asset class, such as stocks, or when holdings in an asset class are concentrated in a particular sector or even the stock of a single company. If, for example, most of your assets consist of stock holdings in an automotive company or a worldwide beverage producer, or the stocks of only a few companies, or even your own long-time employer, your account is not diversified. Similarly, if your account includes stocks, bonds, and equity mutual funds that are primarily in the technology or energy industries, for example, your account is not diversified. In the event your investments decline in value, your broker might be held liable for failure to diversify your account.

If your broker tells you, for example, that companies in the oil and gas industry are poised to achieve record earnings, and that you can realize a greater rate of return by focusing your investments in this sector or by investing in one or two particular stocks or equity mutual funds, the broker is breaking the cardinal rule of investing. Your risk of losses—which can occur rapidly—increases dramatically in an over-concentrated account. Diversification is an essential element of any successful investment strategy, and your broker has the duty to help you achieve this goal.

However, many times, investors themselves are to blame for an over-concentrated portfolio.

Our law firm represented dozens of WorldCom employees who had their entire life savings wrapped up in WorldCom stock before it imploded. The same thing could happen to a friend of mine should something go wrong at GE. If it did, and my friend decided to sue his broker on the basis that he should not have been over-concentrated in GE stock, he would have a hard time convincing an arbitration panel that the broker was at fault. After all, my friend wouldn't have sold the stock anyway. If you are in this position, you should think hard about this issue and try to separate the emotional attachment to the stock from the harsh reality that you are setting yourself up for financial suicide, particularly if you are retired or on the verge of retirement.

—*Contributed by Jason Doss*

Lesson 38————————————

The Perils of Company Stock

If concentrated stock portfolios are bad, buying your employer's stock either inside or outside of your retirement plan makes it even worse.

There are dumb investments, and then there are *really* dumb investments. Employees that buy any more than token amounts of company stock have signed up for a great deal more risk than they need to.

The general rule that diversification is good doesn't stop at the company fence. A diversified portfolio helps protect investors against all the things that could go wrong that you can't even imagine today. Any first-year finance student knows that diversification carries no penalty in return reduction. Diversification is as close to a free lunch as investors can hope to find. Concentration of investments is bad, leading to higher risk without any higher expected return.

But, the problem of employer stock inside of any kind of pension plan is particularly acute. Economists make a distinction between investment capital and "human capital." Human capital is the value that the individual brings to society and may be (very roughly) measured in lifetime wages. Human capital is a "wasting" asset. It's also a risky asset—once it's gone, it's gone. The flying fickle finger of fate can intervene at any time. At least some human capital must be converted to investment capital over time. That's why you set up retirement plans, buy life and disability insurance, and save.

Another problem with human capital is that it is difficult to diversify. Because few of us can manage more than one career at a time, it makes sense to diversify away from the employer risk in your investment capital. After all, if your company does poorly, some employees (or all of them) might find themselves out of a job at the same time that their stock is in the tank.

You have all seen major failures, such as the Enron, Global Crossing, and dot.com blowouts. History repeats itself with devastating frequency. Why take that risk?

It's easy for employees to deny the problems of the employer, or think that they have "insider" knowledge of the company's position. Many of those Miami employees were buying company stock right up to the day the doors closed. In fact, employees are often carefully kept in the dark to keep up morale. To ensure an orderly liquidation, Eastern kept information under wraps right up until the hour they shut down. Employee briefings are not held to the same standards that analyst briefings are.

A Pan American captain was counseled a while ago that when a company's bonds are selling for less than the amount of the next interest payment, the market is saying something about the likelihood that the dividend will be paid. He bought them anyway. The rest, as they say, is history.

But even healthy, high-growth companies can experience dramatic swings in their stock prices, subjecting employees' finances to gut-wrenching roller-coaster swings. An employee recently confessed on TheStreet.com that his 401(k) balance was 70% invested in employer stock, and before he could roll it over when he left, it fell more than 50%. Ironically, he went on to say that his former employer, Charles Schwab, would be the first to warn against concentration in any single stock. "I have a bunch. But…my account doesn't look so hot," he said.

Companies often make stock available to their employees at a discount. This discount can take the form of incentive stock options, and discount stock-purchase plans. It's easy to see the advantages for the employer: increased loyalty and identification with corporate goals by the recipients, reduced payroll costs, and even a reduced cost of capital. Start-up companies often finance their operations with "funny money" stock options.

But it's a mixed bag for the employees. On one hand, there may be something to be said for turning employees into rugged capitalists. On the other hand, it defies the logic of diversification and compounds the problem by lumping the human capital of your job into your investment capital. Still, these employees are supposedly making informed free-market choices. Of course, you have all heard about the millionaire employees at Microsoft. Microsoft employees have won the lottery. But, for every one of them, there are hundreds of employees laboring away with company stock that is going nowhere. Investing is not about winning the lottery; it's about building security and reducing risk.

It's shocking that Congress allows corporations to fund their retirement plans with company stock. Tax-qualified retirement plans are supposed to be for the exclusive benefit of the beneficiaries, and fiduciary standards should apply. Employees trapped in pension plans requiring funding with company stock should complain to management and write their elected representatives.

How much of your employer's stock should you own? Maybe zero. Employees who hold more than a token amount of their employer's stock do so at their peril. If you are offered it as an option in your pension plan, decline. If you already own some, sell it at the first opportunity. If it is held by your pension plan, the fiduciaries are not doing their job properly (just ask the employees of US Air). If it comes as a "match" in your plan, diversify at once.

Recognizing the Effect of Volatility

Monte Carlo simulation and today's powerful spreadsheet applications give us far more insight into the problem, and point out some additional solutions that would not have been possible with historical back-testing.

Simply put, *Monte Carlo simulation* utilizes random draws of numbers from pools constructed with specified rates of return and volatility (risk). Much like a lottery, you build a pool of numbers and pull them out at random to construct a single test. Then you repeat the process 1,000 or 10,000 times and summarize the results. The summary provides a quantitative estimate of the range and distribution of the possible returns. By varying the construction of the pools of numbers, you can examine different strategies to see which ones give a higher probability of success.

For instance, you could construct pools of numbers that have an average return of 10% and a standard deviation of 10%. Then, starting with a $1 million dollar portfolio, you can test the survival rates of 4%, 5%, 6%, and 7% withdrawal amounts 1,000 times each. Your findings will generally confirm the Cooley, Hubbard, and Walz study.[1]

For example, run the tests again using a pool of numbers with a 10% rate of return but a standard deviation of 10%, 15%, and 20%, and a withdrawal rate of 6% per year. At 30 years, only 1% of trials fail at 10%, but 23% fail at a standard deviation of 20%. Failure rates soar with the higher volatility! All 10% returns are not equal (see Figure 38.1).

---

[1] Cooley, P. L., Hubbard, C. M., and Walz, D. T. (1998), "Retirement spending: choosing a sustainable withdrawal rate," *Journal of the American Association of Individual Investors*, 20(2), 16-21.

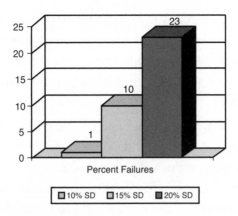

Figure 38.1   Percent failures

The simulation reveals a clear link between volatility and survival of the portfolio at any given time horizon. Anything you can do to reduce portfolio volatility (given the same rate of return and withdrawal rates) significantly enhances the chance that a retiree's nest egg will survive.

Totally Skewed

In the traditional analysis described previously, you might think that half of all trials would result in greater-than-expected returns, and half would result in less-than-expected returns. But, it's worse than that. The only case where each trial yields the average result occurs where there is no portfolio volatility. In that special case, every trial survives and gets the identical result.

With volatility, outcomes become skewed. Even though you obtain the expected rate of return across the sample, the median return is less than the average. The higher the volatility, the greater the sample becomes skewed at any time horizon. So, while you get the average return you expect, the average result is less than what you expected. As the number of failures goes up, the number of extraordinary results also goes up. A small number of players obtain results that are much higher than expected, while a large number of players' portfolios either fail or obtain lower-than-expected results.

For example, suppose you expect a terminal value of $100,000 for a particular withdrawal rate, rate of return, and time horizon. If one result yields $1,000,000, and nine results yield $0 at some particular risk level, you have achieved your average return. But, nine of ten retirees are broke!

The relationship between risk and reward only works at the asset-class level. It doesn't work for individual stocks. In theory, two stocks with similar characteristics will have similar returns. They do have identical expected returns, which may be based on historical returns of similar assets, but in fact are just guesstimates. The very second you rate them, they begin to change. One may be wildly successful, while the other may tank. That's the kind of risk that can be completely diversified away. And here's the kicker: You won't get an additional return (compensation) for any risk that you could have diversified away. All you get is extra risk if you fail to diversify properly—and nobody ought to take an uncompensated risk.

A poorly diversified portfolio picks up a boat-load of risk and no additional compensation. A single stock picks up a supertanker load of uncompensated risk. Because your chances of beating the market are very poor, and because you are certain to generate unacceptable risk by selecting individual stocks, they should have no place in your portfolio.

The investor's job is to pare away ruthlessly any uncompensated risk. You won't be compensated for individual company risk, industry sector risk, and country and regional risk. You won't be compensated for management risk. The way to diversify prudently is to buy the entire market—and the entire market is the world market, not just the U.S. market, as many U.S. investors seem to believe.

Rather than set out to generate the highest possible return regardless of risk, let's define the portfolio as the one generating the highest probability of reaching your goals.

See the "Web Extra" articles on the importance of managing risk, how much risk you should take, and how it influences your probability of success at www.Sink-Swim.com.

Lesson 39 —————————————

Taking the Right Amount of Risk

One of the most important advances in modern financial theory goes by the unlikely name of Tobin's Separation Theorem. It greatly simplifies the way you should think about investing, and directly affects the problem of retirement planning. Starting with the idea that somewhere out there is a perfect equity portfolio, you must assume that anybody in the world who wanted a risky portfolio would want that portfolio. It's the one with the highest possible return per unit of risk out of the infinite portfolios we could possibly construct. We refer to that as the *Super Efficient Portfolio*.

Then you must recognize that not all investors will want exactly that amount of risk and, additionally, they have liquidity needs that make them want to hold different portfolios.

A few investors will crave additional risk and return potential. They can simply leverage the Super Efficient Portfolio by buying it on margin. In general terms, most of us don't want to go there. This is an area reserved for wild and crazy guys.

For some, the Super Efficient Portfolio is just the right amount of risk and return possibilities. A well-diversified, equity-only portfolio might be appropriate for someone with a long-term time horizon and a tolerance for market risk.

Many investors need liquid assets set aside to pay upcoming obligations, or simply prefer a lower amount of risk. For instance, they might want to buy a house next year, or send their daughter to Harvard in three years. Or, perhaps they need a store of value to fund the next few year's known retirement income needs.

They can temper their portfolio by adding a very low-risk component like short-term, high-quality bonds. In essence, these investors will hold two portfolios: a risky one and a riskless one. The difference between investors is how much of each they should hold to meet their exact requirements for risk, reward, and liquidity preferences. For the rest of the book, I am going to call this the "two bucket" portfolio solution.

If you have a very long time before you need to spend some of your portfolio, you might very well decide to hold an all-equity portfolio. What do you care how much it goes up and down if you don't need the money for an extended period and want to achieve market-level returns?

As you get closer to your goal, you are going to begin to care about market fluctuations. So, you will want to lighten up on the risky bucket and begin to fill up your low-risk bucket. How much should be in your low-risk bucket? I would say that anything you expect to withdraw from your investment accounts over the next seven to ten years should be in the low-risk bucket. The balance can be reasonably safely kept in the risky bucket to provide for long-term growth and generate market returns.

You might think of this as the "glide slope" approach to asset allocation. There is a range of reasonableness around the glide slope to accommodate people with different risk tolerances. But, generally, it should be a useful guideline to keep people from taking too little risk early in their careers, and too much risk later on.

For example, let's say that you want to be in your perfect retirement portfolio five years before your desired retirement date. That's a good idea because you don't want the decision about retiring tomorrow to depend on what the market did yesterday. Further, let's say that you plan on a 5% withdrawal annually from your account and that you would like to have at all times an eight-year reserve of known withdrawals available. By multiplying 5% by 8 years, you get a 40% weight in short-term bonds. Your glide slope might look like Figure 39.1.

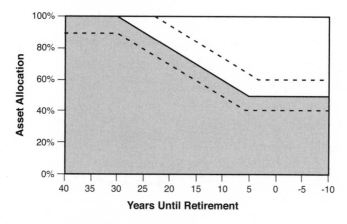

Figure 39.1   Asset allocation glide path

Refer to the chart every five years as you count down to retirement and make the necessary adjustments to your two-bucket asset allocation.

Assuming a very simple asset allocation of 40% domestic stocks, 40% foreign stocks, 10% real estate, and 10% commodities futures in your equity bucket, Table 39.1 shows suggested asset allocations as you progress through your career.

Table 39.1   The Glide Slope: Example of Suggested Asset Allocations

	40 Years	30 Years	20 Years	10 Years	5 Years	Retirement Years
Domestic	40%	40%	32%	28%	24%	24%
International	40%	40%	32%	28%	24%	24%
Alternative	20%	20%	16%	14%	12%	12%
Bonds	0%	0%	20%	30%	40%	40%
Totals	100%	100%	100%	100%	100%	100%

Here are a few general principles first. Later, you will see some examples of how to implement these principles for different situations. You should apply these principles to all your investments, both inside and outside your qualified plans. Your aim should be to craft one comprehensive investment scheme that includes all your assets.

Effective investment policy can be summed up very easily:

- **Equity.** Passive management, global diversification, a tilt toward small and value, further diversification with real estate and commodities futures.

- **Fixed Income.** Short-term, high-quality bonds. If foreign, hedged against currency risk.

- **Risk Tolerance and Time Horizon.** Match the mix between equity and fixed income to your unique financial situation, objectives, time horizon, and risk tolerance.

Lesson 40

It's the Portfolio, Stupid!

Modern finance is all about moving from a solution based on individual securities to a portfolio solution. Building an investment program on a stock-by-stock basis rarely works.

The appropriate solution is to divide your investments into two buckets: a risky (stock) bucket, and a risk-free bucket (short-term bonds of high quality). The first decision an investor needs to make is how much to put in each bucket. Start by identifying all the cash flows that the portfolio must support for the next several years. That's the minimum for your bond bucket. All the rest might be put into risky assets if that doesn't exceed your risk tolerance. Otherwise, put more into your bond bucket until you can sleep well at night. But, almost all investors need to have enough risky assets growing to cover inflation and meet their reasonable financial goals.

Each of the two buckets must be as "efficient" as possible. An efficient portfolio is one that has the maximum return per unit of risk.

Here is a mind-blowing intuition. The most efficient portfolio of stocks (equity) is the one that every person on the planet should want to hold. It's the best possible portfolio, so all investors who want any risk at all will want to hold it. Keep that idea in mind, because we will be back to it.

Lesson 41

Traditional Active Managers Are a Waste of Money

Individual stock selection and market timing decisions are a highly effective way to increase costs, reduce returns, and increase risk.

Market Efficiency

Markets are efficient, which means that security prices quickly reflect all available news and information about a company. A few million reasonably well-informed players reach a consensus value for the stock almost instantly. This does not mean that the stocks are "correctly" priced, only that playing the stock market is a very hard game to win, if you think that you can consistently pick winners or spot losers often enough to overcome the costs of trading and doing the research. The implication of this is that hiring a manager for individual stock selection is a waste of time and money, and leads to a lower expected return than just buying the market as a whole. To make the situation even worse, trading individual stocks generates taxable transactions that the investor must bear. Trading causes a huge tax drag because the net taxable transactions are reported to the IRS for each shareholder once each year. Think of it this way:

Expected Net Return = Market Return – (Costs and Taxes)

A few managers will beat the market. Somebody always wins the lottery, too. But the expected return of a lottery ticket is horrible. Those few managers who "beat" the market during one period are no more likely to beat the market during a subsequent period than any other manager. If we pick the right benchmark, beating the market is not a game of skill so much as pure, dumb luck. Pure, dumb luck is not a good strategy for anyone looking to optimize their probability of a good result.

Beating the market is not a reasonable objective. Capturing the vast majority of market returns is a reasonable objective. Market returns are quite bountiful, and it's an easy thing to capture them.

Here is the trade-off: Attempting to beat the market by traditional stock selection/market timing will reduce average returns by 1% to 2% per year while increasing the risk. But, the chance of beating the market is somewhere between 20% to 30% during any given timeframe. That's a sucker's bet.

Randomness

Market prices are random. Fortunately, they are random around a core value that is positive. Random means that they are impossible to predict. Of course, if they were possible to predict, we could all get rich just timing the market: get in on the good days, get out on the bad days. How sweet that would be. Unfortunately, markets are driven by new news, which in itself is impossible to predict. News arrives randomly, and securities prices react to it randomly.

Manager Effectiveness

Because markets are efficient and random, it's a total waste of time and money to hire a manager either to time the market or pick individual securities. In fact, manager risk—the risk that the manager may make bad selections—adds an entirely new level of uncompensated risk that you don't need. Fortunately, you don't have to hire managers to capture market returns. So, don't.

Build a Global Portfolio of Asset Classes

If managers are unlikely to add value, what should you do?

The alternative and preferable technique is simply to use index funds or ETFs that replicate asset classes. This provides for the lowest cost, lowest risk, and lowest tax profile *within the asset class*.

Lowest risk needs to be taken in context of the asset class. Clearly, a small company index fund has substantially higher risk than short-term bonds, but if your strategy calls for an allocation to small companies, buying the entire asset class is the lowest risk position for the class. Remember, it's asset-class exposure that drives returns.

Asset-Class Investing

The overwhelming factor that explains portfolio performance—both risk and return—is its exposure to various asset classes. If you simply know the portfolio's exposure to stocks, bonds, and cash during any particular time period, you can tell what its return was.

The more finely you define asset classes, the better your estimate of returns will be. So, for instance, in the U.S. stock market, you could define large companies, micro-cap companies, and value and growth companies. You could do the same for foreign-developed and emerging markets. Additionally, you could include real estate and commodities futures as asset classes in the equity bucket.

Bonds can be broken down by asset class according to their duration (time to maturity) and their credit risk. If you are considering foreign bonds, you must account for additional currency risk, or hedge it away.

Lesson 42

Investment Vehicles

Today's market offers a mind-boggling menu of choices to build your portfolio. Only a few of them are worth considering, and some are truly toxic.

Individual Stocks and Bonds

Forget what Jim Cramer says. Individual stocks and bonds have no place in your portfolio. It's delusional to believe you can beat a half billion of your closest friends in the game of trying to outguess the market. All you will accomplish is lowering your probability of success and carrying a boat-load of risk you don't need.

Mutual Funds

The best way to achieve economical diversification in an asset class is to pool your money with other investors by purchasing a mutual fund.

Separate Accounts

Unless you have more than $50 million to place in a single asset class, a separate account is a waste of money. All you will get is a more expensive, less effective mutual fund.

Index Funds

Index funds are a special type of mutual fund that skip the management question and simply buy all the stocks in an asset class in proportion to their importance (as measured by relative value of the shares outstanding) in the asset class.

An *index fund* is a traditional, open-ended mutual fund that seeks to replicate the performance of a selected index. Purchases and sales take place directly between investors and the fund. Pricing is fixed for both transactions at the close of business each trading day when the Net Asset Value (NAV) is determined. Because all transactions occur between the fund and individual investors, the fund must maintain a portion of its assets in cash to provide for liquidity, and redemptions might cause tax implications to remaining investors. In practice, this theoretical tax issue has never been a problem.

Exchange Traded Funds

Exchange traded funds (ETFs) trade like a stock, but otherwise look almost exactly like a mutual fund. However, their operating expenses are usually significantly lower than the traditional index mutual fund. Lower expenses are a good thing indeed, and, if you have a choice between identical indexes, go for the one with the lowest cost.

The explosion of product offerings in the ETF universe offers investors viable alternatives to the traditional index mutual fund.

Although relatively new, the growth curve is staggering. The ETF has been embraced by both institutions and individual investors, and has unique characteristics that make it attractive to both markets. Certainly, ETFs will be a potent force in future markets.

Although there are significant differences, both offer passive investing, low cost, tax-efficient, pure-market exposure that replicates closely a widely followed index. In short, either are excellent choices for an investor seeking to build an effective asset allocation plan.

ETFs and index funds are so much alike that, for many uses, they are almost interchangeable. For long-term investors, the most significant considerations might be expenses and acquisition costs. Because such costs vary from firm to firm and plan to plan, investors have to make an assessment of their unique situations.

In general, because ETFs have fewer customer support costs, they can offer lower expense ratios than an index fund. (This isn't always the case, however, so check the fund's prospectuses.)

On the other hand, many index mutual funds can be acquired without commission or other cost. But, the commission costs to acquire ETFs can be significant. For instance, if you make small repeat purchases of ETFs, you might incur enormous transaction costs relative to a direct purchase from a no-load mutual fund family and you might not re-capture such costs through lower fees in any foreseeable timeframe.

Annuities: Just Say No!

There are two kinds of annuities, fixed and variable. One looks like a CD in performance, and the other looks like a mutual fund. Both offer awful tax treatment, horrible internal expenses, and high commissions for the salesperson. Neither belongs in your portfolio. There is never an excuse to place an annuity inside a qualified plan or IRA.

Do-It-Yourself

www.Sink-Swim.com

How Much Will an Annuity Cost You? There is almost no chance an annuity is right for you. After extra fees and confiscatory tax treatment, you wouldn't want one if the claimed extra features were free (they aren't). See how much more an annuity will cost you than a mutual fund without annuity treatment.

It's just about impossible to build a case for annuities that makes economic sense. The most widely sold variable annuities have total annual expenses close to 3%. Contrary to most sales literature, the taxation of annuities is not favorable when compared to a reasonably tax-efficient mutual fund. The tax treatment on distribution is so bad that even if the annuity features were free, you wouldn't want it.

Just say no to annuities! The loss of capital gains treatment and additional annuity expenses eat up more than the benefit of deferral in almost any reasonable case you can make up.

Trust Wall Street to come up with a bundle of really bad ideas and toxic products for the unwary. Stay away from index-linked annuities and CDs, hedge funds, and venture capital funds.

Annuities Should Not Be Sold in Qualified Plans

The main benefit of qualified plans, such as 401(k)s, 403(b)s, and 457s, is that they are "qualified" for income tax deferral under the Internal Revenue Code. In other words, you do not have to pay income taxes every year on the gains in those investments. You pay taxes only when you make withdrawals.

In addition to qualified plans, the main selling point of variable annuities is that they also provide tax-deferred growth. Knowing this, you might think that very few variable annuities would be sold in qualified accounts. Not true, says the National Association of Variable Annuities (NAVA); 50% of all variable annuities (billions of dollars) are sold within qualified plans every year.

Selling variable annuities inside of qualified accounts has been the subject of intense debate and criticism within the financial and legal communities. Like all investments, variable annuities have benefits and costs. Opponents say that variable annuities, with their surrender charges on withdrawals and high expenses, are just too costly, and are little more than "mutual funds" in an overly-expensive annuity wrapper. Proponents of variable annuities say they are superior to equivalent mutual funds because of the tax-deferral feature.

Variable annuities should never be sold in qualified accounts because there are so many other less-expensive ways to invest. At arbitration hearings, it is also very difficult for the broker to justify a recommendation to sell a variable annuity inside of a qualified account. For example, I once represented a retired elementary school teacher in an arbitration where $480,000 of her IRA funds were invested in a high-risk, equity-based variable annuity. The arbitrators found in her favor and awarded her $353,000. Brokers are under a legal duty to recommend investments that are suitable for the investor's financial situation. Determining the suitability or unsuitability of a variable annuity is a two-step process: (1) the variable annuity as a whole must be suitable; and (2) the sub-accounts that contain the actual investments must be appropriate as well. In the client's case, the arbitrators concluded that the variable annuity as a whole was unsuitable, in part, because it was in an IRA, and that the sub-accounts were unsuitable because they were invested in high-risk equities when the school teacher needed a reliable source of income.

Notice that even though she won, the arbitration panel did not award her all of her damages. That is very common in arbitrations. As mentioned earlier, even when customers win, they do not always get 100% of their money back. The client had all the fixings of a great client. She was sympathetic, honest, unsophisticated in investing, and she trusted and relied on the brokers. The panel apparently apportioned some responsibility to the poor, sympathetic client and awarded her less than she was entitled to receive. This is a prime example of why it is so important for you to educate yourself about investments and avoid becoming a victim in the first place.

—*Contributed by Jason Doss*

A Truly Toxic Product

Some financial products are so bad that they have no reason to exist except to fatten the wallets of the companies that manufacture them and the salesmen who peddle them. Unfortunately, even products that might gag a maggot routinely slip through the cracks of our very porous regulatory system. Is there a product so rapacious that it shocks the conscience of an insurance company? Apparently not!

In my opinion, equity-indexed and variable annuities top the list of bad investments. These products are insurance policies masked as investments. They have drawn a lot of heat from regulators in recent years because they are frequently peddled by insurance agents at free lunch seminars. Because equity-indexed annuities, also known as fixed-indexed annuities, currently are not considered "securities" under the federal and state securities laws, these complex products can be sold by any insurance agent licensed to sell life insurance. Variable annuities, on the other hand, are securities and must be sold by salesmen licensed to sell investments. Watch out for these products!

Over the last 10 years, the brokerage and life insurance industries have been battling each other to win the war on baby boomers. The name of the game is selling investments that provide upside potential and at the same time provide downside protection. Brokerage firms have traditionally sold stocks, bonds, and mutual funds. These are the types of vehicles that come to mind when you think of "investments." On the other hand, when you think of "investments," life insurance does not immediately come to the minds of most Americans. Most people think of term-life and whole-life insurance, right?

To eliminate the traditional insurance stereotypes, life insurance companies in the last 10 years have made a push to sell life insurance that resembles investments. In general, these companies accomplish this by combining mutual funds with life insurance.

What do you get when you mix traditional investments with life insurance? The answer is usually annuities.

You should be careful with these products because they are very complex and more costly than traditional investments. Not coincidentally, these products pay higher commissions to brokers and insurance agents than traditional investments, such as mutual funds and traditional life insurance. For example, agent commissions on equity-indexed annuities commonly exceed 10%. By way of comparison, mutual funds typically pay commissions of less than 5%. In my opinion, high commissions drive the sale of these products, not customer demand for what they offer. Most experts agree it is cheaper to purchase investments and life insurance separately.

The complex nature of these expensive products should be a red flag to all investors. One of the golden rules of avoiding becoming a victim of investment abuse is:

Never Invest in Things That You Do Not Understand!

Annuities are so complex and disclosure is so poor, red flags are easy to spot once you know how to identify these products.

—*Contributed by Jason Doss*

Lesson 43 ────────────

Building Your Buckets

The Risky Bucket

As previously stated, the appropriate diversification standard is the world market of stocks. Of course, you can't buy them all, but you can buy most of them through domestic, foreign, and emerging market index funds. Although it might appear riskier to buy foreign stocks than domestic ones, when mixed with domestic stocks in some appropriate ratio, the risk in the portfolio decreases quite nicely. You can accomplish this by buying just two Vanguard index funds. How's that for simple?

A more sophisticated strategy incorporates different risk factors into the portfolio with the intention of spreading risk beyond the traditional stock markets. These risks are different, but not cumulatively greater. A 20% weighting for alternative investments like real estate and commodities futures is certainly reasonable.

Real estate adds valuable diversification to a portfolio. It doesn't behave like a stock or bond but has competitive long-term returns. Because you can buy every traded Real Estate Investment Trust (REIT) through the Vanguard index fund, an allocation to real estate should improve your portfolio risk-return characteristics.

Finally, an allocation to commodities futures might make a lot of sense. Like real estate, the pattern of returns is very different from stocks and bonds, but the risk-reward characteristics are favorable, and they can help to lower the risk at the portfolio level.

Thus far, you are 40% domestic stocks, 40% foreign stocks, and 20% alternative investments. As a basic design, that makes a pretty good portfolio. But, depending on the size of your portfolio and availability of products, you might want to divide each major segment further.

Because investors are systematically compensated for investing in small and distressed companies (value), you might profitably consider overweighting your portfolio with small and value stocks. Again, you can accomplish this with just one or two index funds in the domestic market. It's harder to find foreign small and value index funds or exchange traded funds, but with the explosion of product in exchange traded funds, I expect them momentarily.

Here is a very simple way to execute a portfolio that should be effective over the long haul.

The underlying strategy is to split the world's traditional stock markets evenly into foreign and domestic. That reduces risk and provides for a dollar-neutral hedge. If the value of our dollar goes down a percent, our foreign holdings go up one percent even if they don't move on their local exchange. Then alternative investments such as real estate and commodities futures deserve a place. So you might split the portfolio 40% domestic stocks, 40% foreign stocks, and 20% alternative investments.

You can do the whole thing with one account at Vanguard or two if you have IRAs or pension accounts with their funds available. The criteria are that it be effective, low-cost, low-risk, and low-tax-exposure. Additionally, it's simple to administer and you should get one, consolidated statement. You can do the whole thing with just one account at Vanguard that invests in several of their funds. Go to www.Vanguard.com, and you can set it up online.

As a good start, index the entire world equity market using these two funds:

- Index all the U.S. market using the Vanguard Total Market Index (VTSMX).

- You can index most of the world's foreign markets, including emerging markets, using Vanguard's Total International Stock Index (VGTSX).

Do-It-Yourself

www.Sink-Swim.com

REITs are a great way to diversify an equity portfolio. They have enviable returns and don't correlate to stocks or bonds, which means they have a strong diversification benefit: Vanguard REIT Index Fund Investor Shares (VGSIX).

Over the long haul, small and value companies should outperform the total market. Adding the following two funds will "tilt" the portfolio in that direction. Over time, you should expect a non-trivial return enhancement:

- Vanguard Value Index Fund Investor Shares (VIVAX)
- Vanguard Small-Cap Value Index Fund (VISVX)

As illustrated in Figure 43.1, you might weigh them as follows:

- 20% REITs
- 40% Total Foreign
- 20% Total Market Index
- 10% Value
- 10% Small-Cap Value

This asset allocation plan can be called a Very Good Portfolio (VGP). These risky assets can be purchased from Vanguard in a single mutual fund account. It meets all the criteria discussed previously: economical, effective global diversification; passive management; tax sensitivity; and easy implementation.

The total weighted average cost (expense ratio) of the funds is 0.252% or 25.2 basis points. One really has to wonder why anyone would consider a less-diversified portfolio with higher costs. This portfolio makes a very good benchmark against which to compare your pension plan. Is it worth up to 3% of your total account balance to get an inferior selection of funds inside a 401(k)/403(b)/457 plan when you can build your own portfolio so easily yourself. The tax advantage of the qualified plan quickly gets eaten by the obscene level of annual costs.

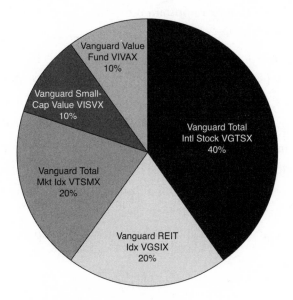

Figure 43.1 Asset allocation risky assets

A slightly more sophisticated approach includes a commodities futures account through the iShares Exchange Traded Fund GSCI Commodity Trust (GSG). Split the REIT allocation down the middle. You will need a brokerage account to hold the iShares; again, Vanguard is a great custodian. You also could use Schwab, Fidelity, or TD Ameritrade, to name just a few.

As your account grows, you might consider using an independent registered investment advisor. The advisor has access to better products than are available to retail clients. But make sure the advisor you choose agrees to a passive global asset allocation strategy, and that additional services are appropriately priced.

As additional asset classes become available in either the traditional no-load index fund or ETFs, you might want to include them. Presently, there are no retail index funds for foreign small companies, foreign value companies, or foreign small value companies. These asset classes are also not available for retail investors in emerging markets. As they become available, work them into your foreign allocation to capture that extra premium that small and value have above the market over the long term.

We are just beginning to see foreign real estate becoming available in REIT-like investment shares for institutional investors. However, they are just over the horizon, and when they become available to retail investors, you might want to split your real estate allocation.

These more exotic asset classes add both an incremental return and risk reduction to the portfolio, but they come at a slight increase in cost. Presently, our private client portfolios include these institutional funds and have a total cost at the fund level of well under 0.5%. Effective global asset allocation doesn't have to be expensive.

The Low-Risk Bucket

Bonds provide a store of value to meet known future expenditures and to lower the risk of the portfolio. Anything they earn is a bonus. This isn't the place to stretch for additional returns by taking additional risk because it's not likely to be compensated. Bond yields can only be enhanced by taking additional risk of quality or duration. But the trade-off stinks. Stick to high-quality, short-term domestic bonds. I would suggest an average duration of two years or less. If you want to take risk, take it on the equity side where it is likely to be compensated. Use a short-term, high-quality bond index for the part of your portfolio that should not be risky. You can do this with one index fund like the Vanguard Short-Term Bond Index Fund Investor Shares (VBISX). The expense ratio is a modest 0.18% or 18 basis points. There is no reason to pay more for a bond fund, as it will simply reduce your returns.

You have to decide the proportion of equities to bonds based on your time horizon, risk tolerance, objectives, and financial situation. The ratio changes as you go through your career, generally becoming more conservative as you approach your expected retirement date.

If your income tax bracket is above 30%, and your bond portfolio is held outside of a tax-exempt account (IRA, pension plan, and so on), you might consider a municipal bond portfolio instead. Again, it should be short-term and high-quality—for example, Vanguard Limited-Term Tax-Exempt Fund Investor Shares (VMLTX).

Do-It-Yourself

www.Sink-Swim.com

Municipal Bond Tax Equivalent Yield: Should you be using municipal bonds? Income generated from municipal bond coupon payments are not subject to federal income tax and often are exempt from state taxes. Use this calculator to estimate the tax-equivalent yield (TEY) for a municipal bond.

Lesson 44 ———————————

Periodic Maintenance

After you have set up the "perfect" asset allocation plan, you can kick back and relax for a while. But, eventually, you will have to do a little maintenance. Over time, your various asset classes will grow at different rates. So, your "perfect" plan will get a little warped.

As in everything else about investing, there are guidelines, suggestions, and considerations, but no hard rules. As an investor, you have to examine your own situation and come to your own conclusions. I am assuming here that there is no life event that would force you to re-examine whether the asset allocation plan was still suitable.

You should re-balance to keep the original asset allocation plan in order to hold risk constant. For instance, suppose that your original plan called for 30% short-term bonds, and 70% equities. If you do nothing, you must presume that the equities will outgrow the bonds over the long haul. As the percentage of stocks rise, the character of the portfolio changes. Although a higher loading in equities may be good for long-term performance, it will place the portfolio at increasingly higher risk.

A side benefit of re-balancing is that it forces us to buy low, and sell high. Over time, you should expect a small, but measurable profit as a result of this "diversification benefit." This works particularly well in well-diversified, multi-asset class portfolios that I recommend.

You should look at both taxes and transaction costs before you decide on your rebalancing strategy. Hyperactive trading is unlikely to add value. Benefits of an absolutely "perfect" asset allocation could easily be consumed by additional costs.

Here's a strategy you could use for starters: Once a year, check to see if any asset class varies from its target weight by more than 3%. If so, consider re-balancing inside any qualified plans first to save taxes. In smaller accounts, or if the total amount of the transaction is small, you might decide to let it just ride. A large number of $50 transactions are unlikely to impact your end result positively.

A natural and painless time to re-balance is whenever there is a cash flow to the account. Whether you are depositing or withdrawing, check to see which classes are out of line and use the cash flow to move back toward "perfect."

Lesson 45

Investing During Retirement

Investing **during** retirement is completely different from investing **for** retirement. Conceptually, at least, it's easy to structure an accumulation program. But the game changes at retirement. Both economically and psychologically, the stakes get higher. Time is no longer on your side. With no more salary coming in, there is no way to make up for investment mistakes. Risk takes on an entirely new meaning. The pucker factor is up.

Here is how you can put to work the principles you learned earlier to solve this critical problem.

There are no average years in the market. Although over the long haul, the market generates enormous wealth, in the short term, it can get pretty ugly. Be prepared for it.

Investors must assess both the probabilities and the potential consequences of their strategies. For example, you know that if you play Russian roulette with the typical revolver, you have but a one in six chance of losing. Unfortunately, although the probability of losing is low, the consequences of a loss could ruin your whole day. The consequences of failure for a retiree, while not quite so absolute, are still unacceptable. Nothing can turn those golden years into a nightmare faster than being broke.

Given the near certainty of occasional market crashes, the wide variation of investment returns in the short term, and the consequences of failure, retirees must adopt strategies with the highest probability of success. They will want to build in a little extra pad for safety. The market neither knows nor cares whether you have retired. It can go down at any time, and stay there for several years. You must maintain adequate liquidity to withstand a few bad years in the market without liquidating your variable assets.

As if the problem weren't already tricky enough, you must expect at least modest amounts of inflation. So, your income requirement will grow throughout life. The longer your time horizon, the more inflation will eat into the buying power.

The trick is to generate at least the required minimum return at the lowest possible risk level. Too little risk, and the portfolio may not generate enough return, whereas too much risk may "blow up" the portfolio during a string of bad years.

During the accumulation phase, it is completely rational and consistent to take a full measure of global equity risk in return for the probable higher returns. The emphasis is correctly placed on attaining the highest possible accumulation. So, early in your career, your glide slope will heavily weight equities.

At retirement, the objectives change: Generate income, and don't run out of money. An entirely different strategy is necessary. The requirement to generate liberal, consistent, and reliable income over a long-term, indefinite time horizon changes the problem in a fundamental way. Withdrawals introduce the distinct possibility that a poorly managed retirement account may self liquidate. The glide slope will still require equities to generate long-term growth to fight inflation. However, you will need a healthy dose of fixed income to reduce the risk and provide a store of value during the inevitable market downturns.

Most investors find that amortization can't work because they can't predict their life expectancy. In this instance, amortization refers to withdrawing a certain percentage of your nest egg each year in the expectation that it will reach zero after a predetermined number of years. The calculation is the same for a fixed interest mortgage.

People often say that the best plan is to die happy having just spent their last dollar. But amortization is out of the question. The time horizon of one's retirement is long and not easily predicted. After all, if you plan to spend your last dollar at your average projected life expectancy, what happens if you screw up and live another five years? Remember that, by definition, half of all people will live longer than the average. In any event, over long periods of time, amortization doesn't add much to income. The additional return of principal isn't much over long periods. Even if you don't care whether there is anything left over for the kids, there's no alternative to keeping the principal intact.

Up until retirement, new checks usually arrive with great regularity. Most will be consumed, a little saved for that far-off day. There is always time to make up for an occasional bad investment decision (not true at all, but that's the way we all seem to feel about far-away events).

One day, the nature of the entire game changes irrevocably. Retirees know that they won't have any chance to make up for poor investment decisions. Whatever they have accumulated is going to have to last forever. In one sense, time has run out. In another sense, time seems to stretch out without limit. The natural inclination is to stop taking any risk at all.

But, there is a strange paradox at work. The avenue that offers the highest probability of achieving long-term financial goals is not the one with the lowest risk.

Several factors complicate the retiree's problem:

- Fixed-dollar withdrawal programs increase investment risk and introduce the possibility of self-liquidating the portfolio during extended market declines.
- Time horizons are extended, but cannot be predicted exactly in advance. According to an IRS table, the average life expectancy for the survivor of a couple age 60/55 is 32.3 years. And half of those couples will have a survivor who lives longer. (It's a unisex table. The IRS can be a little strange at times.)

Do-It-Yourself

www.Sink-Swim.com

Life Expectancy: This calculator can give you an idea of your life expectancy based on your current age, smoking habits, gender, and several other important lifestyle choices.

- Inflation is embedded within government policy. You cannot count on it going away. So, you will have to account for it in your planning. Otherwise, over an extended retirement period, a fixed income will waste away to practically nothing.

Decision-making is complicated by high degrees of uncertainty. Most of the factors that determine success or failure are beyond your direct control. Retirees cannot control or predict market returns, interest rates, or even their own mortality. So, you must focus on the things that you can control, and devise a conservative investment strategy that will yield the highest probability of success.

It goes without saying that a very conservative withdrawal rate increases the chance of a secure retirement. That's the one factor that's directly within the retiree's control.

Because no two retirees have identical situations or objectives, each case must be individually considered. A comprehensive approach will consider all the complicating factors before reaching a solution. No single facet can be considered in a vacuum. The process is a little like putting together a puzzle with many parts. Some compromise may be necessary, and retirees must face up to the possibility of mid-course corrections.

During retirement, a much more conservative portfolio is generally required. That's because the need to generate periodic withdrawals to produce income introduces a risk that the portfolio might self-liquidate. Generally speaking, a retirement portfolio should be very heavily weighted in short-term bonds, which provide a store of value-to-fund needed distributions without interruption and to reduce the risk for the portfolio. Both are important to retirees.

A low-risk, low-volatility portfolio generally provides a higher probability of success during the withdrawal phase than a more volatile portfolio. Here we define success as not running out of money while alive. Although bonds may not earn as much as stocks over the long run, they serve to reduce greatly the portfolio risk.

Let's look at how an appropriate asset allocation between stocks and bonds solves the problem of providing liberal withdrawals, hedging inflation, generating real growth, and managing risk at the same time through the appropriate asset allocation strategy and investment policy.

Every step of the investment policy must support the retiree's objectives. The ideal policy will support the required withdrawal rate while maximizing the probability of success.

The first problem retirees face is that "guaranteed" investment products are unlikely to provide sufficient total return to meet their reasonable needs. Meanwhile, equities are far too volatile to provide a reliable income stream. Because at least part of the portfolio will be volatile, the question of risk management moves to the forefront. A compromise must be reached. A combination of stocks and bonds will probably best meet the needs. The "two-bucket" portfolio meets the needs by allocating funds between the safe and risky assets.

Bucket One—Adequate Liquid Reserves

Recognizing that equity investments are too volatile to support even moderate withdrawal rates safely, investors must temper their portfolios with a near riskless asset that lowers the volatility at the portfolio level and be available to fund withdrawals during down market conditions. As a minimum liquidity requirement, I suggest high-quality, short-term bonds sufficient to cover seven to ten years of income needs at the beginning of retirement.

A generous cushion of bonds provides a ready source of funds for distribution without regard to market fluctuations. Retirees should determine their total income needs for the next seven to ten years and allocate enough bonds to cover at least that amount. For instance, retirees who expect to withdraw 4 percent of their nest egg each year would want to hold at least 28 percent to 40 percent in bonds (see Figure 45.1). With that cushion established, the retirees can withdraw for a very long time without being forced to liquidate their more volatile stocks during a possible down market. It's important to preserve those volatile but high-return growth assets for future recovery.

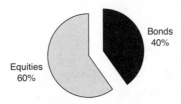

Figure 45.1   Asset allocation: divisionbetween equities and fixed income (bonds).

Bucket Two—World Equity Market Basket

The second bucket contains an approximate weighted world equity market basket. The design philosophy is to construct the equity portfolio with the highest possible return per unit of risk. Equities provide the long-term growth and inflation hedge that the retirees need over the balance of their lives.

Withdrawal Strategy—Preserve Volatile Assets in Down Markets

A rational withdrawal strategy recognizes that equities are volatile and short-term bonds are not. So, you should employ a specific strategy designed to protect volatile assets during down-market conditions. Otherwise, excessive equity capital will be consumed during market downturns.

Most advisors have been content to treat retirement assets as a single portfolio. For instance, many would advocate a "lifestyle" portfolio composed of 60% stocks and 40% bonds. However this leads to withdrawals on a pro rata basis from both equity and fixed assets regardless of market experience. It does nothing to protect volatile assets during down markets.

A far superior alternative strategy would treat the equity and bond portfolios separately, and then impose a rule for withdrawals that protects equity capital during down markets by liquidating only bonds during "bad" years. During "good" years, withdrawals are funded by sales of equity shares, and any excess accumulation is used to re-balance the portfolio back to the desired asset allocation. This approach yields a substantial incremental improvement by imposing this simple rule. However, it does require short-term deviations from the "ideal" retirement portfolio. A few down-market years tilt the portfolio strongly toward equities. However, the strategy provides time for the equities to recover without having to liquidate them during the market declines. In essence, you are imposing a "sell high" discipline on the portfolio.

Importance of Asset Allocation

You may recall that in the late 1990s, all financial professionals seemed to agree that the road to riches involved owning technology stocks. In early 2000, the "road" turned into a "bubble" that burst, destroying the financial future for millions of Americans. During the period, a diversified portfolio meant that you owned 20 different technology stocks. Shortly after the tech wreck officially sunk, Wall Street touted the importance of prudent investing and protecting your nest egg. In the last couple of years, unfortunately, the "stock picking" television shows have resurfaced. So, what is the point? Wall Street has a short memory, and the next "road to riches" investment is right around the corner. Don't fall for the marketing hype.

You can make just as much money and sleep a lot better by investing your money in both fixed income and equities. The appropriate mix of these categories can accomplish your goals and give you the flexibility to weather the next meltdown.

In the last few years, our firm has represented many clients whose investments were inappropriately handled because they were advised to put all of their eggs in stocks. None of their investments were in bonds or cash and, as a result, the account was too risky for their investment needs.

Thousands of investors filed lawsuits to recover their investment losses on this basis, but they were in the minority. Only a fraction of the total victims ever filed suit or thought to speak to an attorney simply because they did not know that they could take recourse against a brokerage firm. Remember that you have legal recourse as a victim of bad investment advice.

—Contributed by Jason Doss

Lesson 46 —————————————

Selecting an Advisor

Avoiding Advisor Risk

Market risk and behavior risk are well-known and frequently discussed. However, there is another type of risk that is often overlooked: advisor risk.

Investors who recognize that they don't have the time, knowledge, or inclination to deal with market risk, or the discipline to deal with their own behavior risk, might seek advice and unwittingly run into a third level of risk: the risk that their advisors are either not working in their best interest or are incompetent. This risk is little discussed or appreciated. But, advisor risk is not trivial. Countless investors who delegated their investment decisions to so-called professionals have been devastated during the recent bear market.

You should start by asking yourself for whom the advisor works. The world of investment advice is dominated by sales organizations including brokerage houses, broker-dealers, insurance companies, mutual funds, and banks. These firms hire salespeople to sell high-profit (for the firm) products. The salespeople are compensated by commissions that are based solely on the economic interest of the firm. There is only one ethic: Sell more! Any gains realized by the investor are a pure happy coincidence. Failure to sell enough of the "right stuff" is a career-ending move for these captive salespeople. As my friend Bill Bernstein says: "Brokerage houses service clients like Bonnie and Clyde serviced banks."

These houses offer advice worth far less than zero and, far too often, operate at a level little better than common thieves in pin stripes. From top to bottom, the commission-based system is fatally flawed, hopelessly corrupt, riddled with conflicts of interest, hidden agendas, and lack of disclosure. Too often, the totally predictable result is inappropriate investment recommendations, churning, proprietary products, high costs, and dismal results. These problems are a direct result of Wall Street's moral vacuum and its well-demonstrated inability to police itself.

The conflicts of interest involved in commissioned sales taint the entire brokerage service model. It's a sad fact that the least attractive, highest cost, highest risk, and most complicated investment schemes pay the highest commissions to the broker. Guess what they want to sell?

Perhaps you suffer from a lingering doubt that Wall Street's brokerages are working for you. If so, you can quickly disabuse yourself of that delusion. Simply review Henry Blodget's stomach-turning email file obtained from the New York State Attorney's investigation of Merrill Lynch.

Why would any investor subject himself to the risk that his advisor is not working exclusively in his best interest? Why would you pay to obtain advice that isn't objective? Commissions introduce a totally unnecessary moral risk into the advice function.

The large Wall Street brokerage houses each spend more than the total GDP of many African nations every year on marketing to convince you that they are a trusted source of investment guidance. But, if you are looking for honest, competent advice, keep in mind that their incentive is to maximize their own commissions and the firm's profits. Additionally, in spite of fancy titles, the average broker is a used stock salesman with little clue about the modern financial theory of portfolio construction.

There is a simple alternative that eliminates that problem. Just refuse to deal with any commission-based advisor. Commission-based compensation includes "fee-based" compensation, which is a particularly evil label referring to *both* fees *and* commissions. Don't be fooled.

Investors must insist that the advice they receive is totally objective, and exclusively in their interest. Independent fee-only registered investment advisors (RIAs) provide advice and service. Their compensation is paid directly by the client, fully disclosed, completely transparent, and product-independent. With the commissions gone, there is nothing in the relationship that prevents the advisor from providing objective advice.

The investor's best defense against inappropriate advice is the ironclad separation between the advice and brokerage functions. The advisor works only for the client, receives no other compensation, and as a fiduciary acts only in the best interest of the client. The National Association of Professional Financial Advisors (NAPFA) fiduciary pledge sets the standard for advisor conduct. Ask your local used stock salespeople if they will sign it. From the client's perspective, no other relationship is acceptable.

NAPFA FIDUCIARY OATH:

The advisor shall exercise his/her best efforts to act in good faith and in the best interests of the client. The advisor shall provide written disclosure to the client prior to the engagement of the advisor, and thereafter throughout the term of the engagement, of any conflicts of interest which will or reasonably may compromise the impartiality or independence of the advisor. The advisor, or any party in which the advisor has a financial interest, does not receive any compensation or other remuneration that is contingent on any client's purchase or sale of a financial product. The advisor does not receive a fee or other compensation from another party based on the referral of a client or the client's business.

Most brokerage houses will not allow their brokers to sign this oath, even if they are dual-registered as RIAs. They simply will not agree to act in the client's best interest! So much for their objective advice claims.

Getting Objective Advice

It is possible to get objective competent advice, but you need to know where to look and for what to look. Look for a fee-only advisor that has no financial arrangements with any product provider. Then expect to pay him or her directly for their advice. They will usually work under either an hourly fee, annual retainer, or a percentage of assets under management arrangement. Paying for advice directly eliminates the conflict of interest where the advice may tilt toward "yield to broker" rather than maximizing your portfolio value.

A pure heart and an empty head are not enough either. Finding the right fee-only advice requires you to look hard at the individual's professional qualifications. Absent a few felony convictions, almost anyone can become a registered investment advisor. They are not all created equal.

A quick review of the firm's SEC required disclosure forms (ADV Parts 1 and 2) gives you a lot of information about the firm and its operations, qualifications, regulatory history, investment philosophy, fees, assets under management, and time in business (http://sec.gov/investor/brokers.htm).

You don't want to entrust your financial future to a rookie. Experience counts. A degree or graduate degree in finance, economics, or business is a good foundation for this industry.

There are a only a few professional designations and associations worth considering, as follows:

- The CFP™ mark, which requires a rigorous course of study and then continuing professional education in most of the elements of personal finance that surround the investment decision (www.cfp.net).

- Membership in the National Association of Professional Financial Advisors (NAPFA) signifies a fee-only advisor who meets minimum experience and educational requirements and most importantly adheres to a fiduciary standard (ww.napfa.org).

- The ACCREDITED INVESTMENT FIDUCIARY™ signifies advance study of fiduciary practices (www.fi360.com).

- Finally, Paladin Registry pre-screens financial advisors for high competence, experience, and ethical standards (www.paladinregistry.com).

There is an entire universe of additional designations of very limited value that planners award themselves. They may look good on a business card, but they don't add anything to competence.

Finally, it's imperative that the investment policy of an advisor is economical, effective, and tuned to your exact financial situation. You might ask how the suggested portfolio compares to our Very Good Plan (VGP) in terms of total cost, service, diversification, level of risk, and probability of success. If you don't like the answers you get, move on. After all, it's your money—you have to sink or swim, you are the person who drowns if the plan fails, and you have to be comfortable with the advisor and the strategy.

Who Is the Lifeguard on Duty?

Financial advisors are like lifeguards in that you are paying them to keep you out of trouble. However, picking a good financial professional is not an easy task because all of them seem to have an alphabet soup list of credentials and designations next to their names. It is very hard to separate the experts from the idiots.

The first rule of picking your financial professional is to ignore all of their designations because they are little more than marketing tools designed to capture your trust. Some designations are more difficult to obtain and may point you in the right direction, but even a "lofty" CFP (Certified Financial Planner) designation does not ensure that you will receive advice that is appropriate for you.

Next, you need to be aware that there are basically two categories of financial professionals: registered investment advisors and registered representatives. By statute, investment advisors have an unquestionable fiduciary duty to act in the best interests of their clients. Advisors are required by federal and state law to disclose all conflicts of interests and give unbiased investment advice. On the other hand, the scope of a registered representative's fiduciary duty depends upon the relationship with the client, how that financial professional holds himself out to the public, and an array of other considerations.

The most important thing to know is that, should you ever have to file a lawsuit to recover your losses, registered representatives are the defendants that deny... deny... deny that a trust relationship existed or that they owed you any fiduciary duty at all. As I said before, in this circumstance, the scope of the once-clear trust relationship is often reduced to a he-said, she-said dispute.

Investment advisors, on the other hand, cannot legally minimize the scope of the trust relationship because there are statutes that clearly spell out their duties to clients. For this reason, it is best for anyone who intends to rely on the advice of a financial professional to do so only with registered investment advisors or insist that the financial professional you are dealing with commits in writing to be a "fiduciary" on your account. Obviously, not all registered representatives are bad. You just shouldn't trust someone with something as important as your money (and pay them handsomely) only to have that registered representative's lawyer deny that they owed you any duty when something goes wrong. Eliminating any dispute about the scope of the broker's fiduciary duty equates to better settlements and larger arbitration awards. This is called the duty-based approach to picking a financial professional.

Beware that just because you have an account at a well-known brokerage firm does not mean that your broker is a registered investment advisor or is always acting in the capacity of a registered investment advisor. In fact, such firms employ both investment advisors and registered representatives and, at times, their brokers wear both hats. The easiest way to spot registered investment advisors is to look at their business card or letterhead. It will identify them as an RIA, short for registered investment advisor. Don't solely rely on those indicators, though. Ask them point blank: Are you a registered investment advisor? Are you a fiduciary on my account? If so, please confirm it in writing. You can also contact your state securities regulator and verify the information.

If you find out that your current broker is not an RIA, either get rid of him altogether or, if you like the job he is doing, protect yourself by writing him a letter to confirm the nature of your relationship. If you are like most people and completely rely on your brokers "expertise" for making investment decisions, confirm it in writing. At least you are creating a record and brokerage firms are required by law to keep all correspondences in your file. As with all important issues that you face in life, however, it is best practice always to make copies for your own records as well.

The third step in selecting a financial advisor is to check out their background for prior disciplinary action and lawsuits before you invest with them. The good thing about the securities industry is that it is highly regulated, so every lifeguard leaves a footprint in the sand. A financial advisor's disciplinary history and employment history is collected and recorded in a Central Registration Depository (CRD)/Investment Advisor Registration Depository (IARD). The information on this system is public record, and you can retrieve it easily either by pulling a BrokerCheck report on the www.finra.org website or by contacting your state securities regulator. In my experience, I have found that the state CRD/IARD reports are more complete than the reports available on the FINRA website. If brokers are not registered on the CRD/IARD system, then they are not licensed to sell securities and, in my opinion, you should not hire them.

Pulling a CRD/IARD report is a very important and easy way not only to gain control of your financial future, but also to avoid bad brokers altogether. For example, a broker once called me and, based on his sales pitch, was obviously trying to set up an in-person appointment so that he could sell me a variable annuity. After his first call, his CRD/IARD report was obtained, which showed that he had only been in the business for two years. Of course, he called a second time as a follow-up call. While on the phone, he was pressed about reasons not to buy a variable annuity (there are plenty) and, in an attempt to gain trust and show his expertise, he said that he had been in the business selling investments with his firm for more than six years. This was a blatant lie, given that his CRD/IARD stated that only three years ago, he was selling pizza at Papa John's Pizza. (No offense to Papa John's.)

His CRD report helped me stay in control of the telephone conversation because I knew more about him than he did of me. Everyone should follow this example. The more information you know, the easier it is to cut through the sales pitches and make good decisions.

Recognizing the Red Flags of Securities Account Mismanagement

There are an infinite number of ways that a shark can bite you. However, there are some common warning signs. Existence of one or more of these warning signs does not always mean that you have been bitten, but further inquiry is strongly recommended.

That list includes the following:

- The client's initial contact with the broker was through a "cold call."

- The client is vulnerable to suggestions or pressures exerted by the broker due to age, infirmity, lack of sophistication, or other similar factors.

- Whether sophisticated or not, the client does not understand the nature of the investment the broker has purchased.

- The broker uses high-pressure tactics to obtain client approval for trades or purchases.

- The broker makes promises of high returns coupled with low risk.

- The broker claims to give the client access to investment opportunities normally available only to very wealthy or otherwise well-connected investors.

- The broker ignores or disparages client's stated investment objectives and risk tolerances.

- The broker places trades without the client's prior permission.

- The account statements reflect a high level of activity, with securities often being held for short periods of time.

- The portfolio is overweight in volatile stocks in the technology, biotechnology, internet, energy, or other "hot" sectors.

- The account has significantly underperformed benchmarks, such as the Dow Jones Industrial Average or the S&P 500 Index.

- The account statement reflects risky investments, such as volatile stocks, derivatives (options, futures, foreign currency), micro-cap stocks (small companies with unfamiliar names), and bulletin-board stocks (not listed on major stock exchanges—so where are they?).

- The cash balance reflected on an account statement unexpectedly shows up as a negative number, usually meaning securities have been purchased on margin.

- Unexpected withdrawals of cash, particularly by wire transfer.

—*Contributed by Jason Doss*

Lesson 47

Reaching Your Goals

Personal Savings and Liabilities

If Social Security and your pensions aren't enough to keep you afloat, then the rest has to be made up from your savings and investments. It's no secret that Americans are not saving much. The only studies that showed that Americans were even close to on track with their retirement savings included the value of their homes as retirement assets. And although Americans thought that the value of their houses would only go straight up, it's highly unlikely that we can all become independently wealthy by trading our houses with one another.

www.Sink-Swim.com

Do-It-Yourself

Retirement Shortfall: Running out of your retirement savings too soon is one of the biggest risks to a comfortable retirement. Use this calculator to find a potential shortfall in your current retirement savings plan.

Although private investment accounts don't offer all the advantages of deferred taxation that pensions and IRAs do, they have the most flexibility. You will have ultimate control over how your funds are invested, when they are deposited and withdrawn, and how much to contribute. Properly constructed, a private investment account can be very effective, low-cost, low-risk, and tax-efficient.

Do-It-Yourself

www.Sink-Swim.com

Taxable vs. Tax-Advantaged Investments: This calculator is designed to help compare a normal taxable investment, a tax-deferred investment, and a tax-free investment.

But only you can save. No one else is likely to do it for you. You can conceivably save money in one of two ways:

1. Spend carefully, perhaps guided by a master plan and budget process, and then save what's left over.

2. Save first, and then spend what's left over.

Method one sounds great. But, it just plain doesn't work! It will fail with about 99% of the people who try it.

In the first place, budgeting isn't fun. Who are you kidding? Can you in your wildest dreams imagine sitting down once a month to pour over your household spending? Would you even want to hang around with someone who enjoyed doing the family budget? Forget it. It's not going to happen.

Budgeting sounds great in theory, and someplace there is a highly disciplined ascetic monk who can stay within his budget. But, for the rest of us, there are just too many temptations.

There is always a new putter that will improve our game, a new scuba regulator that will breathe easier at 100 feet, a new camera lens that has a more powerful zoom, new restaurants to try, a more stylish suit, sexy new shoes, or cuter baby clothes. You get the idea. As long as there is a positive balance in the checkbook, it's hard to say no to ourselves, our spouses, or our children. At the end of the month, nothing is going to be left.

The very best way to do this is to put your money into a good qualified plan. You get some nice tax benefits, protection against creditors, and a shield against your own temptation. The tax penalties and aggravation of making a pension withdrawal are enough to keep a person with a modicum of self-discipline honest.

If there are no qualified plans available to save in, or if your plan is so bad that no reasonable person would invest in it, use IRAs. Then have money direct-deposited from your payroll account into a mutual fund company, with the balance going to your household checking account. If your company won't do a payroll deduction, have it deducted from your checking account on the first day after it's deposited. The trick is to make it automatic. You shouldn't have to think about it. It should just happen like magic. What doesn't pass through my hands doesn't get spent. It's out of sight and out of mind.

There are, of course, two further steps in order to reach our objectives: Invest prudently, and don't raid the piggy bank. On the subject of raiding the piggy bank, you have to be firm with yourself. Once it's in your long-term savings and investment account, you must convince yourself that it doesn't exist anymore. Mentally, you must build an impenetrable wall between yourself and your nest egg.

Seriously, saving first works. It is not an accident that many peoples' largest financial asset is their retirement plan. Why do you suppose that is? Because the money is invested automatically before they get to spend it, and there are substantial obstacles between them and the money. These obstacles provide just enough discipline to ensure that the money stays at work for them. If you keep "borrowing" from your nest egg for foolish little indulgences, it's not going to grow to make you financially secure.

Remember, you are in a sink or swim environment. If you don't do it, no one is going to do it for you. So, put your savings on autopilot, relax, and enjoy the trip.

You Must Save Early, Lavishly, and with Discipline

The game plan is pretty clear: Invest early, invest lots, and invest in a diversified portfolio of equities to get reasonable long-term performance.

Experience has shown that an investor saving between 10% to 15% of pre-tax income over a working career can achieve economic security at retirement. If you have decent qualified plans available, then maxing out your contributions to IRAs, 401(k)s, profit sharing, or pension plans should go a long way toward meeting the goal. Current tax deductions and tax-deferred compounding make the whole process both more efficient and somewhat less painful. But, remember, the tax treatment is just the icing on the cake. Save and invest you must, or be prepared to eat dog food during retirement.

If the concept of spending somewhat less than your total income plus credit-card limits is foreign to you, you may want to consider the alternatives. Failure to attain your retirement goal will result in delayed retirement or drastic cuts in your lifestyle. Those second-career elderly that McDonald's is so proud of probably aren't flipping hamburgers because they burned out on golf and sailing!

The sad truth is that Americans are saving less than at any time since the Great Depression. Department of Commerce reports consistently show that (excluding pensions, IRAs, 401[k]s, and so on) the savings rate of U.S. consumers falls to zero or below. Not a good sign during the longest economic expansion in memory. Baby boomers might want to rethink their consumption habits.

Do-It-Yourself

www.Sink-Swim.com

Benefit of Spending Less: Reducing your spending can be worth more than you might think. Use this calculator to see just how much your budget reductions may be worth.

Lunch Savings: Use this calculator to see how a simple change such as bringing a bagged lunch to work can really add up.

Cool Million: Find out when your savings plan might make you a millionaire!

Don't Delay Your Savings! Waiting to begin your savings plan can have a huge impact on your results. This calculator helps show you how much postponing your savings plan can really cost.

Keep Time on Your Side

Time is such a valuable commodity; it's a shame when investors squander it. Yet many investors blow it, wasting a resource that can't ever be recovered.

Time is an investor's most valuable ally. Account balances increase *exponentially* over time, which is as close to magic as most of us will ever see. Putting time on your side is a key element to financial success.

Do-It-Yourself

www.Sink-Swim.com

Compound Interest and Your Return: This calculator demonstrates how compounding can affect your savings.

Time is a finite commodity for all of us. Once it's gone, it's gone. There is no getting it back. So, putting time on their side should be a top-level concern for all investors. It's never too early to start a long-term investment plan.

Investors who understand just how valuable time is will want to *keep* time on their side. An avoidable investor mistake can fritter away years of savings and effort, placing you right back at the starting point with little or no time to recover.

Avoid these common mistakes to keep time working for you:

- **Do not raid the retirement account.** A disappointingly huge percentage of workers fail to roll over their pension and profit-sharing accounts when changing jobs. The funds are used for everything from vacations to new cars. It's especially important to keep all your retirement accounts at work. Although the amounts might seem relatively small, if left to accumulate tax deferred in an IRA, they will grow to substantial amounts. For instance, $10,000 left to grow at 8% for 30 years will be worth $100,626 when it's needed for retirement.

---

www.Sink-Swim.com

Do-It-Yourself

401(k) Spend It or Save It Calculator: There are several ways to manage your 401(k) when you leave an employer. Making the wrong decision can cost you thousands of dollars, both in taxes and lost earnings.

- **Do not take a flier.** Some delusional investors rationalize that a series of high-risk investments will average out over time, and that a loss today can be made up by tomorrow's gains. These serial losers buy into one deal after another that sounds too good to be true, hoping for a huge payoff. This gambler's mentality has almost nothing to do with investing, and rarely leads to anything but financial ruin.

- **Do not over-concentrate investments.** Anything less than a fully diversified portfolio magnifies risk without increasing expected return. No investors should ever bear a risk that could be diversified away. They can't afford for all or a large portion of their savings to vaporize. The more concentrated a portfolio, the more opportunity for something awful to happen. Just ask any Enron employee how they like their company stock now. Avoid sector funds, individual stock holdings, and funds with concentrated positions.

Keeping your funds in play with reasonable investment strategies and constant discipline is just as important as starting early. Blowing up your nest egg along the way destroys your most valuable ally in the quest for financial independence.

But, the real trick is to plan and have the discipline to save. Hope is not an action plan! You, and only you, can make it happen.

Please don't say that you can't afford to save anything—most people find the money if they want a new car or stereo. You might spend that much for your morning jolt of cafe latte. Do you really want to be a millionaire? Or, do you just want somebody to give you the money? (Hint: It ain't gonna happen.) You decide.

How much will it take you to make your goal? Check out our goal calculator at www.Sink-Swim.com. To run the calculator on your web browser, you need Microsoft's Internet Explorer Version 4.01 or higher with the Office Tools installed. All this can be downloaded for free from the Microsoft website.

---

www.Sink-Swim.com

Do-It-Yourself

Investment Goal Calculator: Are you on track for your goals? Use this calculator to see if your investment plan is on track to meet your investment goals—and receive suggestions on how to change it if you are falling short.

If you want the spreadsheet, you can download it from our website. You need Microsoft Excel installed on your computer.

Lesson 48 ————————————

Public Policy Issues

Social Security

In a Ponzi scheme, money is shuffled to a few "winners" from early "investors," who in turn will be paid off by later investors—that is, until the whole scheme collapses under its own weight. There is no real business. As long as enough new money can be attracted, all is well. But, eventually, the scheme runs through the supply of gullible new investors, and the predictable meltdown occurs. Substitute "beneficiaries" for "winners" and "taxpayers" for "investors," and you have Social Security.

There is not one single penny in the Social Security trust fund. The government simply steals the surplus intended for other purposes. When the surplus disappears, the shortfall will have to come from general taxes.

In October 2007, the Treasury Department estimated the Social Security shortfall at $13.6 trillion. They suggested a 25% cut in benefits and a 50% increase in taxes might delay its collapse. That, my friends, is only the beginning. You can expect the retirement age to go up, additional taxes on benefits, and means testing.

Do-It-Yourself

www.Sink-Swim.com

Social Security Benefits: Use this calculator to estimate your Social Security benefits.

How Important Is Social Security? Use this calculator to determine how losing this important retirement asset could affect you.

Make no mistake—the plan as it is currently operating is going to crash without major overhaul. It's only a matter of time. With no political will to fix it, the implication to you is clear. Don't plan on Social Security being a major part of your retirement income.

Our fathers and grandfathers were lifted out of poverty by Social Security. The political reality is that Social Security will always be there. The economic reality is that it won't provide nearly as much as it did for our fathers. You can expect that if Social Security is your only asset, you will be mired in poverty.

You can request a tailored benefit estimate from the Social Security Administration online at https://secure.ssa.gov/apps6z/isss/main.html. You also can calculate your own at http://www.ssa.gov/OACT/anypia/. If you forget the address, just google "Social Security Estimate" and the administration's pages will pop right up.

Medicare

As it stands today, the healthcare system is a total wild card. Absent radical reform, retirees must plan for increased medical expenses that are not going to be covered by employers or the government. The funding for healthcare shortfall dwarfs the Social Security problem and, like Social Security, it's entirely unfunded. Meanwhile, corporations are ditching anything resembling retiree healthcare benefits.

Unless you get some reform, once again you are on your own. So, plan to fund a good deal of the cost of medical insurance and care yourself. That means an extra supply of capital. It's hard to know how much and, unlike long-term care, you might not be able to purchase insurance in advance.

We are in the middle of a great national debate on the future of healthcare. Both Social Security and Medicare are political creations. Write your congressman and senator. Let them know how critical the issue is to your future and to America's future.

Sinking Is Not an Option

You wouldn't have picked up this book if you didn't want to have a safe, secure, and prosperous retirement. You can reach the point where work is optional. At that point, new vistas open up, and your choices become limited only by your imagination. With your economic needs taken care of, you are set to embark on what can be the most exciting stage of your life.

This is an entirely possible dream:

- Save liberally.
- Start early.
- Invest smart.
- Understand your pension plans.
- Use quality tax-deferred plans where available.

Please check www.Sink-Swim.com for calculators, updates, and additional information, such as articles and links to valuable outside resources. Also, read the Sink or Swim blog and join in the discussion group.

Have a great retirement!

Glossary _____

401(k) Plan: A type of profit-sharing plan where employees make contributions to provide for a retirement benefit. The employer might make matching contributions to encourage participation.

403(b) Plan: A defined contribution plan for non-profit institutions.

457 Plan: A defined contribution plan for state and municipal employees.

A

Accrued Benefit: The amount of plan benefits that participants have earned to date in their plan.

Active Management: An investment strategy that relies on a manager to make individual stock selection or market timing decisions in the hope of outperforming an index or other investment benchmark.

Annuity: Any series of payments. However, in common usage, the term refers to an insurance company investment product that offers a guaranteed lifetime income as one of its features. Both the income and the investments might be either fixed or variable. Fixed returns or payments are guaranteed at some level by the insurance company. Variable returns or payments depend on the performance of the underlying investments of the policy. Immediate annuities begin payments at once, while deferred annuities commence payments at some future date.

Asset Allocation: The investment policy decision that divides the portfolio between equities and fixed income, and then further divides the portfolio into various asset classes. Research indicates that asset allocation is the major determinant of portfolio performance.

Asset Class: A group of securities that have common characteristics, which distinguish them from the remaining group of securities. Examples are small U.S. companies, large foreign companies in developed markets, emerging market companies, Treasury bonds, and sub-prime mortgages.

B

Bonds: A security that represents a debt of a business or government. Bonds pay interest at a fixed rate, usually semi-annually, and then repay principal at the maturity date. Beyond interest and return of principal, bond holders do not participate in the profits of the business.

C

Catch-Up Provisions at Age 50: Additional contributions allowed for persons over age 50 to 401(k) plans, 403(b) plans, or IRAs.

CD: A Certificate of Deposit or Time Deposit issued by a bank, credit union, or savings and loan association.

Conduit IRA: An IRA used as a temporary holding place for a rollover destined for another qualified plan.

D

Deferred Compensation Plan: Any plan that results in payments to employees after their termination or retirement. It might be qualified or non-qualified plans.

Defined Benefit (DB) Plan: A qualified plan where the amount of the benefit is known in advance, usually a percentage of final compensation, and the plan contributions by the plan sponsor are adjusted to provide the benefit at retirement date.

Defined Contribution (DC) Plan: A qualified plan where the amount of the annual contribution is known, usually based on compensation percentage, but the final benefit depends on the investment growth of the account. Also referred to as a Money Purchase Pension Plan (MPPP).

E

Employee Retirement Income Security Act of 1974 (ERISA): Also referred to as the Pension Reform Act, it provides the basic framework for regulation of qualified plans.

Exchange Traded Fund (ETF): A mutual fund that trades between investors like a stock rather than having the fund create or redeem units on a daily basis.

F, G, H

Fiduciary: Individuals who manage property for the benefit of another, exercise discretionary authority or have control over assets, are held in a capacity of trust, and render comprehensive and continuous investment advice. ERISA requires the highest level of prudence and loyalty of any of the various fiduciary standards.

Fiduciary Advisor: An advisor qualified to give individual investment advice to plan participants of self-directed plans. This term was created by the Pension Protection Act of 2006 to provide a safe harbor for plans to help participants if certain conditions are met regarding the prudent selection of advisors and controls over their compensation to limit potential conflicts of interest.

Forfeiture: The amount of the accrued benefit that is lost upon termination of employment.

I, J, K

Independent Advisor: An advisor working independently and in the best interest of his clients rather than representing a company or product.

Index: A defined group of investments whose performance can be tracked daily or on a minute-by-minute basis. Indexes serve as a benchmark for investment performance within their defined universe of securities.

Index Fund: A mutual fund that invests in the securities as defined by the index it tracks. Index fund investing is a passive strategy that does not rely on active management to make individual stock selection or market timing decisions.

Individual Retirement Account (IRA): A tax-advantaged retirement plan funded by individuals, or by a distribution (rollover) from a qualified plan. IRAs are not covered by ERISA.

L

Leverage or Financial Leverage: Using debt to buy an asset. Leverage increases both risk and reward dramatically as a small shift in asset price is magnified at the equity level. Examples of leverage include using a credit card, buying a house with a mortgage, and buying stock on margin.

M

Margin: A type of financial leverage where an investor borrows against a security account to purchase more securities.

Money Market Funds: Mutual funds that invest exclusively in very short-term debt instruments. They are designed to provide a competitive yield and cash equivalent safety and liquidity.

Money Purchase Pension Plan (MPPP): The basic defined contribution plan where the plan sponsor makes a contribution to a qualified plan each year, as determined by a formula based on compensation.

Monte Carlo Simulation: A recognized model used to analyze the return and risk that an investment portfolio is capable of producing. It looks at thousands of random investment outcomes that might occur in the future.

Mortality and Expense (M&E): An additional charge for annuity and insurance products that cover the cost of providing an annuity guaranteed rate at sometime in the future. The value of that benefit is close to zero, and the high additional cost simply reduces future accumulations under the contract.

Mutual Fund: A pooled investment account that creates or redeems units for investors at the end of each business day.

N, O

Non-Qualified Annuity: An insurance company annuity that is not part of a qualified plan or IRA.

Non-Qualified Plan: A retirement plan that does not qualify for special tax treatment. These are typically private agreements between the employer and employee. Non-qualified plans do not have to conform to the numerous requirements of a qualified plan, and are therefore more flexible and may result in higher benefits for the employee than a qualified plan.

P

Passive Management: A financial strategy in which the manager is investing in an index or asset class and makes as few portfolio decisions as possible, in order to minimize transaction costs, including the incidence of capital gains tax.

Pension Benefit Guarantee Corporation (PBGC): A government-chartered insurance company that guarantees limited benefits for defined benefit plan participants in the event of a plan failure.

Pension Protection Act of 2006 (PPA): Extends and enhances ERISA by tightening up funding requirements for defined benefit plans, and modifying provisions of defined contribution plans to make them more effective for the plan participant.

Portable: The ability to take accrued vested pension benefits from a plan upon termination of employment.

Profit-Sharing Plan: A type of defined contribution plan where plan sponsor contributions are determined annually, usually depending on profits. However, the plan sponsor might make contributions even if there are no profits at their discretion.

Q

Qualified Annuity: An insurance company policy included in an IRA or qualified plan.

Qualified Plan: A retirement plan designed to meet the qualifications of the IRS code allowing for special favorable tax treatment.

R

Real Estate Investment Trust (REIT): A special stock or equity investment vehicle that holds real estate for investors and receives special tax treatment on rental income or mortgage income, as long as investors distribute at least 90% of their taxable income. REITs trade like common stock, so they allow investors to hold real estate in a highly liquid form.

Required Minimum Distributions (RMD): A schedule of required distributions from qualified plans beginning at age 70½ for retirees or, in the case of beneficiaries, immediately for inherited IRS or qualified plans. Failure to meet the required distribution schedule results in a substantial penalty tax.

Rollover IRA: An IRA that is funded by a transfer from another IRA or qualified plan.

Roth Feature: An alternative taxation treatment available for either 401(k), 403(b), or IRAs. Instead of a tax deduction for a contribution, withdrawals of principal and all accumulations inside the plan can be tax free as long as they have been held for five years and the beneficiary is over 59½. Principal may be withdrawn tax free at any time. Roth accounts are not subject to Required Minimum Distribution (RMD) requirements for the owner and might have substantial estate planning advantages.

S

Section 404(c): A section of the pension law that enables plan sponsors to shed liability for pension investment decisions to plan participants of self-directed plans, making the plan participant responsible for the investment outcome.

Section 72(t): A section of the IRS code that allows for early retirement (before age 59½) withdrawals from IRAs and qualified plans without the normal 10% early withdrawal tax penalty. Three different calculations are allowed to determine the withdrawal amounts, which are sometimes referred to as Substantially Equal Periodic Payments (SEPPs).

Self-Directed Plan: A qualified defined contribution plan where participants are responsible for making investments in their segregated accounts.

Separately Managed Account (SMA): A pooled account for an individual investor. It generally has higher expenses and might have less diversification than a mutual fund.

SEPPs: Substantially Equal Periodic Payments that satisfy the IRS requirements for penalty free withdrawals for persons under the age of 59½ under Section 72(t).

Stocks or Equities: Securities that represent an ownership position in a business. They are entitled to share in profits and losses of the business and increases in the value of the securities.

T, U

Tax-Sheltered Annuity (TSA): Another name for a 457 plan for municipal or state employees. The name is misleading because funding a 457 plan with annuities is not required.

Traditional Pension: Throughout the book, this refers to a qualified defined benefit plan offering steady lifetime income benefits to the retiree.

Treasury Bills: A short-term debt instrument issued by the U.S. Government. Often used to define the zero risk investment standard.

V, W, X, Y, Z

Vested Benefit: The amount of the accrued benefit not subject to forfeiture upon termination of employment.

INDEX

J-K

U

unauthorized trading, 138
underperforming plans, legal
  protection against, 93-94
unsuitable recommendations
  from brokers, 137-138

V

variable annuities, 204-205
variable insurance, 206-207
variance drag, 181
volatility, 190-192
voluntary freezes, 80-81

W-X-Y-Z

Walz, Daniel T., 149
withdrawal rates, sustainable,
  148-151
working in retirement, 15-19
WorldCom, 186

FINANCIAL TIMES

In an increasingly competitive world, it is quality of thinking that gives an edge—an idea that opens new doors, a technique that solves a problem, or an insight that simply helps make sense of it all.

We work with leading authors in the various arenas of business and finance to bring cutting-edge thinking and best-learning practices to a global market.

It is our goal to create world-class print publications and electronic products that give readers knowledge and understanding that can then be applied, whether studying or at work.

To find out more about our business products, you can visit us at www.ftpress.com.